GUITAR WORLD PRESENTS

METALLICA. IN THEIR OWN WORDS.
The inside story of the San Francisco foursome
who rose to become the most dangerous band in the world.
Featuring interviews with James, Kirk, Jason and Lars,
heavy guitar lessons and the ultimate guide
to Metallica collectibles!

From the pages of
GUITAR WORLD
magazine

Edited by
Jeff Kitts, Brad Tolinski
and Harold Steinblatt

Published by Hal Leonard Corporation
In cooperation with Harris Publications, Inc. and Guitar World Magazine
Guitar World is a registered trademark of Harris Publications, Inc.

HAL•LEONARD®
CORPORATION

7777 W. BLUEMOUND RD. P.O. BOX 13819 MILWAUKEE, WI 53213

ISBN 0-7935-8079-X

Executive Producer: Brad Tolinski
Producer: Carol Flannery
Editors: Jeff Kitts & Harold Steinblatt
Art Director: John Flannery
Cover Photo: Ross Halfin

Visit Hal Leonard Online at
www.halleonard.com

Table of Contents

Ross Halfin

Metallica: James Hetfield, Lars Ulrich, Jason Newsted and Kirk Hammett

THE HISTORY OF METALLICA

GARAGE DAYS REVISITED: The story of how a little band from San Francisco, armed only with a couple of cassettes and a nice helping of uncontrollable musical rage, revolutionized heavy metal.

IT WAS THE best of times, it was 1980. Lars Ulrich was depressed. And why not? His parents, immigrants from Copenhagen, Denmark, had turned the high school junior's life in charming Norwalk, California, into a bitter thing. Ulrich's father, a one-time tennis pro on the European circuit, was working hard to transfer his own love for the game to his son. But Lars wanted no part of it; who needed tennis, the anxious adolescent reasoned, when there was heavy metal?

This boy was clearly marching to the beat of a different drummer. In fact, he was learning to *be* a drummer. At first, the melancholy Dane was drawn to the heavy sounds of Deep Purple and Kiss. In time, however, his ear turned to the New Wave of British Heavy Metal (NWOBHM)—the sudden surge of Anglo-metal bands that sprang from the dust of the mid-Seventies punk movement. Bands like Iron Maiden and Def Leppard were the NWOBHM genre's cornerstone, while others—such as Angel Witch and Sweet Savage (guitar virtuoso Vivian Campbell's first band)—released limited-but-influential product before dying out and disbanding.

Ulrich's first drumming idol was Deep Purple's Ian Paice, but with the onset of the NWOBHM, he became enamored of Motörhead's Philthy Animal Taylor and Diamond Head's Duncan Scott. As Ulrich spent more and more time emulating his new heroes, his tennis racket, ignored and forsaken, petrified in his closet.

But the drummer remained frustrated and dissatisfied. American radio waves were dominated by the wimpified metal strains produced by Journey, REO Speedwagon and Foreigner. For an energetic lad like Ulrich, harder music was essential.

In the summer of 1981, Lars Ulrich found himself in Great Britain, joyously walking the heavy metal streets of London. He did the big hang with his favorite English band, Diamond Head, who made an enormous impression on Ulrich with such riff-driven songs as "Am I Evil?" and "The Prince." After spending a glorious month with the band, Ulrich returned home, refreshed and musically invigorated.

Back in the U.S., Ulrich cut a miserable figure in Los Angeles, walking the very same streets as the glam rockers he loathed. But the boy's cultural isolation wouldn't last long, as he soon befriended James Hetfield, a sticker-factory laborer and part-time musician. Ulrich wasted little time turning his new friend on to the obscure European music he worshipped, thereby sowing the seeds of one of the great creative partnerships in the history of heavy metal.

Soon the two friends began toying with the idea of forming a band. Hetfield played rhythm guitar and sang with such local acts as Obsession and Leather Charm. Ulrich played drums—none too expertly, it must be admitted. But what he lacked in expertise he more than made up for in enthusiasm.

But for all Hetfield and Ulrich's youthful exuberance, Metallica might not have come into existence were it not for Brian Slagel, publisher of the influential fanzine *New Heavy Metal Revue*. Around the time Hetfield and Ulrich were considering forming a band, Slagel launched a new record label, Metal Blade. The label was to make its debut with a compilation album, *Metal Massacre*, for which Slagel solicited demos from young, unsigned bands across the country.

Hetfield and Ulrich were galvanized by Slagel's call to head-banging action: If the pair of lanky chums could get a band together by the submission deadline, they could record a song for the album. Ulrich and Hetfield, along with newly acquired lead guitarists Dave Mustaine and Lloyd Grant, churned out a 4-track demo tape of "Hit the Lights," their first song ever.

It's tough to envision "Red Vette" or "Blitzer" emblazoned on the *...And Justice for All* or *Master of Puppets* album covers, yet these are two of the band names considered by Hetfield and Ulrich until another metal fanzine editor, Ron Quintana, suggested the name "Metallica" to Ulrich. As legend has it, Quintana was sitting around with the drummer, trying to decide on a name for a new metal fanzine he was planning. "Metallica" and "Metal Mania" were the final nominees. Ulrich assured Quintana that "Metal Mania" was the title to go with, and stole "Metallica" for the band.

Now that they had a proper name, the Ulrich/Hetfield duo presented their "Hit the Lights" recording to Slagel. Though the track featured a laryngitis-plagued Hetfield on vocals and basement production values, there was no time to re-record the tune—the *Metal Massacre* deadline had come and gone. The track was plopped directly onto the album and released during the summer of 1982. Needless to say, Metallica's debut didn't exactly set the world on fire. Adding insult to injury, the band's name was misspelled on the sleeve as "Mettallica."

Fortunately, "Hit the Lights" was soon re-mixed for subsequent pressings of *Metal Massacre*, with some drastic improvements. Hetfield's voice had recovered, thanks to a steady diet of antibiotics. And Ron McGovney, Hetfield's roommate, was invited to join the band after a crash-course in bass playing. With a solid line-up and the re-mix of "Hit the Lights," Metallica proved to be the highlight of the *Metal Massacre* album, trampling over Ratt, Malice, Bitch, Pandemonium and other featured artists.

The baby Metallica spent the rest of 1982 receiving its baptism by fire on stage. The band performed for the first time on March 14, at Radio City in Anaheim, and soon afterward, the British heavy metal powerhouse Saxon had Metallica open their "Denim and Leather" tour stop in L.A. But the band was mostly limited to accepting embarrassing opening slots, billed under the likes of Steeler and Roxy Roller. They even played Ulrich's Norwalk high school—on a gymnasium stage. Behind them stood a kitchen backdrop, a prop from a school theater production. Hetfield appropriately dubbed the gig, "Metallica in the Pantry."

The Metalli-train really got chugging with the advent of "The Demo Era," during which the band recorded a series of well-realized demo tapes that, taken together, virtually qualify as the first Metallica album. The best known demo was *No Life 'Til Leather*, a seven-song recording produced in late 1982. The perfect antidote to U.S. puff-rock boredom, it triggered a small musical revolution. The recording featured Metallica's first few songs, "Hit the Lights," "The Mechanix" (an early version of "The Four Horsemen"), "Motorbreath," "Jump in the Fire," "Seek and Destroy," "Phantom Lord" and "Metal Militia." Riffs hacked like swords, solos flew like bullets, and Hetfield's unconventional singing style (a high-pitched whine, far removed from his current characteristic growl) gave the band a real British metal sound. Lars wasted no time in distributing the tape to every metalhead he knew, spawning a tidal wave of grassroots support. Fans dubbed copies and sent them to friends who dubbed more copies, resulting in the largest (and loudest) chain-letter the world has ever seen. Metallica was soon the biggest unsigned band on the planet.

NWOBHM had caught on, and in its wake came the "New Wave of Global Heavy Metal," with bands like Mexico's Baron Rojo, Denmark's Mercyful Fate and Japan's Bow Wow and Loudness. New fanzines like *Aardschok*, *Kick Ass Monthly*, *Metal Mania* and *The New Heavy Metal Review* popped up. Nearly every city in the world boasted an alternative radio station that catered to this unprecedented explosion of metal upstarts. Collectors treasured demo and live bootleg trading lists that contained thousands of tapes.

Metallica's next break came in mid-September, when Brian Slagel decided to promote his *Metal Massacre* album by booking Bitch, Cirith Ungol and Hans Naughty into the San Francisco Keystone for a September 18 concert. Cirith Ungol dropped off the bill, and Metallica was asked to fill the slot.

Far removed from L.A.'s glam-rock "freak show" scene, the Keystone was frequented by a large platoon of rabid metal fans, all of whom owned the *No Life* demo and knew Metallica's music riff-for-riff. Assaulted with cries of "Bitch sucks!" and "Mustaine is God!" the other *Metal Massacre* bands could hardly finish their sets. The "Bay Area Bangers" had adopted Metallica as their own.

By the winter of 1982, Metallica had become a regular San Francisco attraction, ripping through numerous sold-out appearances. In L.A. they had gone by the slogan, "The Young Metal Attack." But for their die-hard local fans, Metallica implemented a new catch-phrase: "Metal Up Your Ass," which soon became a statement of faith. The demo *Live Metal Up Your Ass* immortalized the band's November 19, 1982, gig.

One fateful weekend between San Francisco shows, at L.A.'s Troubador club, a bell-bottom clad, bass-playing hulk caught Lars and James' attention. The roaring monsoon of energy was Cliff Burton, who flailed his impressive mane like a janitor waving a wet mop. Hetfield and Ulrich immediately placed him on their "most wanted" list. The Rickenbacker-wielding Burton agreed to join Metallica—on one condition: "Relocate to San Francisco."

With L.A. now dominated by the more commercially accessible rhythms of Ratt and Motley Crue, there was little reason for Metallica to stay in Southern California. Ron McGovney had always been considered a temporary bassist by Hetfield and Ulrich, but when he learned of his bandmates' interest in Burton, he left Metallica an understandably grumpy man.

The new and invigorated Metallica planted itself in El Cerrito on February 11, 1983. Burton debuted with the band on March 15, at the San Francisco Stone. Dubbed "The Night of the Banging Head," the Stone show also featured Exodus' Kirk Hammett, whom fate would bring together with Metallica before long.

Meanwhile, from the primitive interior of a New Jersey flea market booth called "The Rock 'n' Roll Heaven," a bearded mammoth of a man named Jon Zazula was fast becoming the metal godfather of the East Coast, selling rare metal import albums and promoting East Coast concerts. In January of 1983, a denim-and-leather- clad customer visited the booth and slipped a tape of *No Life 'Til Leather* into the store's cassette player. Absolutely pummeled by Metallica's overwhelming sound, the portly Zazula dropped everything, tracked down the band and asked to be their manager.

In March of 1983, as Metallica piled into a rented U-Haul and embarked on a 3,000-plus mile jaunt across the country to play some East Coast dates and meet with their enthusiastic new coordinator, Zazula started phoning major labels in hopes of landing a record deal for the band. When there were no takers, the frustrated entrepreneur reverted to the NWOBHM philosophy of self-production and established his own label, Megaforce.

The band, however, was growing increasingly frustrated with the difficult Mustaine, who drank heavily at times. After several near-fatal road mishaps and internal Mustaine-versus-management scraps, Ulrich and Hetfield decided to give the hard-living guitarist the boot. It was a tough call; Mustaine was regarded by many fans to be the charismatic engine behind Metallica.

"We've decided you're not in the band anymore," announced Hetfield to a barely-awake Mustaine on the morning of April 11. The band was shacked up in Chicago after playing a weekend of gigs. "Well," asked Mustaine, "when does my plane leave?" His now ex-bandmates immediately slapped a Greyhound ticket into his hands.

With a saddened Mustaine en route back to the West Coast (where he would eventually find great success with Megadeth), the remaining Metallica members anxiously awaited the arrival of his replacement that very evening. Prior to Mustaine's actual departure, Ulrich and Hetfield had sifted through numerous demo tapes in search of a new guitarist. When Mark Whittaker, Metallica's road manager at the time, recommended Exodus fretman Kirk Hammett, their ears perked up. Exodus was the Bay area's number-two power-metal property, always nipping at the heels of Metallica. Before doing business with Metallica, Whittaker had managed Exodus, and knew Hammett's potential. Plus, he told Hetfield and Ulrich, unlike Mustaine, Hammett was a regimented and studious string-strangler. Ulrich and Hetfield had planned the whole thing perfectly: Hammett arrived a few hours after Mustaine's departure.

At two a.m. the next morning, at New York's Music Building, the Hammett-era Metallica held its first jam. The three veterans were pleasantly surprised to see that not only did Hammett know their entire repertoire, but that his knowledge of comic book and horror movie lore was exceptional.

Hammett's first gig with Metallica was on April 16, 1983, in Dover, New Jersey. The band worked out the rest of its new-guy bugs during April and May at shows in Massachusetts, New Jersey and New York in support of the Rods, Venom and Motorhead. Metallica then headed to Barrett Alley studios in Rochester, New York, where they recorded their debut album, *Kill 'Em All*, between May 10 and 27, 1983. Some called the music thrash, while others preferred the term "power metal." Whatever the label, Metallica's unique hybrid of sounds represented a whole new genre.

—*K.J. Doughton*, Reprinted from *Guitar World*, October 1991

IN 1984, METALLICA continued their steady rise to the top by touring Europe as the opening act for Venom, and issuing the Europe-only EP, *Jump in the Fire*. After an unsuccessful attempt to get Armored Saint vocalist John Bush to join the group, they headed to Copenhagen, Denmark, to record their second album, *Ride the Lightning*. By the end of the year, Metallica had signed on with Q-Prime Management and Elektra Records and were on their inexorable way to superstardom.

The next year again saw the group hard at work on the road and in the studio. In September 1985, Metallica headed back to Copenhagen to begin work on *Master of Puppets*. Highlighted by its metal-anthem title track and the epic instrumental "Orion," *Master* put Metallica over the top, as it immediately entered *Billboard*'s Top 30, and went Gold soon after. Supporting the album as the opening act on Ozzy Osbourne's U.S. tour in support of his *Ultimate Sin* album, Metallica proved that they could rock arenas with the same energy and stage presence they brought to clubs and smaller venues. The tour was going well until Hetfield broke his arm in a skateboarding accident, leaving him unable to play guitar. After canceling one show, Metallica enlisted their guitar tech, John Marshall, to fill in as rhythm guitarist while Hetfield sang for the rest of the tour.

The group then took a few months off, but Hetfield's arm had still not fully healed. In September Metallica took off on the European leg of the "Damage, Inc." tour, with Marshall handling double duties as guitar tech and rhythm guitarist. Doing both jobs, however, proved to be too taxing for Marshall, who resigned during the tour.

On September 26, Metallica played their first show with Hetfield back on guitar. It also turned out to be their last show with bassist Cliff Burton. That night, on their way from Stockholm, Sweden, to Copenhagen, Denmark, the group's tour bus skidded off the road and rolled over onto its side. Burton was killed.

Years later, John Marshall recalled the scene for author and band authority K.J. Doughton: "Cliff was on the top level of the right rear bunk, and I think that as the bus was bouncing around, he was sort of pushed through the window. Then, when the vehicle fell over on its right side, he was halfway out the window and it fell on him."

"I just recall our tour manager, Bobbie Schneider, saying, 'Okay, let's get the band together and take them back to the hotel,'" James Hetfield told Doughton. "The only thing I could think was, 'The band? No way! There ain't no band. The band is not 'the band' right now. It's just three guys.'"

The group returned home to America, facing the seemingly impossible task of replacing Burton. The charismatic bassist had played a major role in Metallica—not just musically, but in shaping their image, attitude and personality.

A month later, Jason Newsted, who had been playing in a thrash group called Flotsam & Jetsam, joined the group. "Trying to find someone new when Cliff died was like, 'Man, this guy had better be good,' " Hetfield later told *Guitar World*. "We chose Jason because he can write, he's really energetic, and he can down-pick as fast as me!"

After breaking in Newsted with a few months of touring, Metallica released its next studio project, *The 5.98 EP Garage Days Re-Revisited*, a collection of cover tunes the band recorded for fun, intended for their die-hard fans. The unpolished EP sold well, but was deleted from the Elektra catalog after a few years. The band felt it had served its purpose.

In 1988, after recording *...And Justice for All*, which would become their commercial breakthrough, Metallica headed out on the Monsters of Rock tour with Dokken, the Scorpions and Van Halen. The song "One" became an MTV staple—the first significant airplay Metallica had ever received—and the band performed it live on the Grammy Awards.

1991 saw the release of *Metallica*, also known as the "Black Album," on which the band reinvented its sound with the help of producer Bob Rock. Gone were the epic-length songs and "scooped" guitar tones that obscured Newsted's bass playing. "We wanted to create a different record and offer something new to our audience," Hammett said. "I hate it when bands stop taking chances." Those chances paid off; the album shot up the charts on the strength of the singles "Enter Sandman" and "The Unforgiven," catapulting Metallica to a level of popularity all its own among rock bands.

Five years later, with the musical climate completely changed by alternative music, Metallica once again shifted gears with *Load*. With short haircuts and a looser, more melodic sound, the band found a way to flourish in the metal-unfriendly Nineties. "In the time between albums, we watched all this shit fly by and wondered, 'How does Metallica fit into this?' " Hammett told *Guitar World*. "And then we realized that we didn't fit into it at all, never have, and never really will." In the summer of 1996, Metallica supported the album on the Lollapalooza tour, proving they could change with the times without betraying the essence of their music.

—Jeff Colchamiro

GUITAR WORLD, OCTOBER 1991

METAL REFLECTORS

Kirk Hammett and James Hetfield look back on some of Metallica's brightest moments.
By Jeff Kitts

METALLICA'S 1983 DEBUT, the explosive *Kill 'Em All*, taught a grateful world a lesson in unbridled thrashing fury. Since then, their sound has passed through numerous stages, resulting in more than 50 uniquely different compositions. While Kirk Hammett has characterized the hungry band that used to rehearse in a dank garage and today's outfit as being like "night and day," the guttural intensity that was the hallmark of the young Metallica remains the essence of the band today. Evidence of this can be found throughout *Metallica*, the boys' fifth and latest album.

Over the last eight years, Hammett and James Hetfield have established themselves as metal's quintessential guitar alliance. In the following retrospective, Kirk and James take a walk down Metallica memory lane and critique some of the key songs in the band's harsh, noble history.

"SEEK AND DESTROY" *(Kill 'Em All*, 1983)

KIRK HAMMETT: We didn't have a big budget, and everything on that album was rushed. When I listen to my lead now, I hear a lot of out-of-tune notes. Like a bend that just didn't make it and went right over my head because I was so overwhelmed with being in the studio. I used my black Flying V with an old '57 humbucker, which I've had for 12 years now. I plugged in through James' modified Marshall amp, mainly because we didn't have a lot of equipment at that time. I also used a Boss distortion pedal.

JAMES HETFIELD: The idea for "Seek" came from a Diamond Head song called "Dead Reckoning." I used to work in a sticker factory in L.A., and I wrote that riff in my truck outside work. This was our first experience in a real studio. I used a white Flying V, which was the only guitar I had back then. I still have the guitar in storage. The song is based around a one-note riff that was up a little higher. Though most of my riffs are in E, that one worked off an A.

"THE FOUR HORSEMEN" (Kill 'Em All, 1983)

HAMMETT: Prior to recording that song, we put in a slow middle section that wasn't there when I first joined the band, and it needed a slow, melodic solo. I remember going through the song with everyone, and when I got to that part, I played something really melodic. Lars [*Ulrich, drummer*] looked up at me and said, "Yeah, yeah!" He's a big lead guitar fan—one of his biggest influences is Ritchie Blackmore. For that song I put down one lead, then added one on a different track. I wasn't sure which one to use. I listened to both tracks at once, to see if one would stand out. But playing both tracks simultaneously sounded great, and we decided to keep it like that on the record. Some of the notes harmonized with each other, and I remember Cliff [*Burton, bassist*] going, "Wow, that's stylin'—it sounds like Tony Iommi!"

HETFIELD: Dave [*Mustaine, Metallica's original guitarist*] brought that song over from one of his other bands; back then it was called "The Mechanix." After he left Metallica, we kind of fixed the song up— the lyrics he used were pretty silly.

"CREEPING DEATH" (Ride the Lightning, 1984)

HAMMETT: When we first began playing that song in the garage, I noticed that the lead guitar part also incorporated the chorus. I thought that was a good opportunity to play something a bit wild and dynamic. The first figure in that song pretty much came off the top of my head. I was still using the black Flying V and the Boss distortion pedal through Marshall amps, with a TC Electronics EQ. For that song, Flemming [*Rasmussen, engineer*] suggested that I double-track the solo, which made it sound a bit thicker and fuller. We did that solo, after which we had to do this small fill at the end—a four-bar break with four accents afterwards. The plan was to fill the break up and play something over the four accents. When I studied with Joe Satriani, I did this chordal exercise, a diminished chord with four notes. I just played that over these four accents, and it worked out real nice.

HETFIELD: We demoed "Ride the Lightning" and one other song in the studio before we recorded the album. So there's actually a demo somewhere of those three songs with different lyrics. When we did the crunchy "Die by my hand" breakdown part in the middle, I sat in the control room after we did all the gang vocals, and everyone was just going nuts! That was our first real big, chanting, gang-vocal thing—there was almost some production value to it. That whole album was a big step for us. By then I had the Gibson Explorer—I grew to love that shape better than the V.

"FADE TO BLACK" (*Ride the Lightning*, 1984)

HAMMETT: I was still using the black Flying V, but on "Fade to Black" I used the neck pickup on my guitar to get that warm sound. I played through a wah-wah pedal all the way in the "up" position. We doubled the first solo, but it was harder to double the second solo in the middle because it was slow and there was a lot of space in it. Later I realized that I harmonized it in a weird way—in minor thirds, major thirds and fifths. For the extended solo at the end, I wasn't sure what to play. We had been in Denmark for five or six months, and I was getting really homesick. We were also having problems with our management. Since it was a somber song, and we were all bummed out anyway, I thought of very depressing things while I did the solo—and it really helped. I played some arpeggios over the G-A-B progression, but we didn't double track that solo. When that was finished, I went back and did the clean guitar parts behind the verse. James played an arpeggiated figure while I arpeggiated three-note chords. We ended up getting a very Dire Straits-type sound.

HETFIELD: That song was a big step for us. It was pretty much our first ballad, so it was challenging, and we knew it would freak people out. Bands like Exodus and Slayer don't do ballads, but they've stuck themselves in that position, which is something we never wanted to do; limiting yourself to please your audience is bullshit.

Recording that song, I learned how frustrating acoustic guitar can be. You could hear every squeak, so I had to be careful. I wrote the song at a friend's house in New Jersey. I was pretty depressed at the time because our gear had just been stolen, and we had been thrown out of our manager's house for breaking shit and drinking his liquor cabinet dry. It's a suicide song, and we got a lot of flack for it; kids were killing themselves because of the song. But we also got hundreds and hundreds of letters from kids telling us how they related to the song and that it made them feel better.

"MASTER OF PUPPETS" (*Master of Puppets*, 1986)

HAMMETT: I used a Mesa-Boogie Mark 2C amp and a black Randy Rhoads custom Jackson guitar. For the four-bar fill at the beginning of the song, the rest of the guys wanted something high and screeching, but I came up with something a bit more percussive and riff-like, a flatted fifth-type figure. I got this real raunchy, over-distorted sound, which clashed well with the tight rhythm sound James had. James played the first solo in that song, which is a great solo. I worked on the next solo for a couple of days—getting it tight was a real task for me. While recording the track, my hand accidentally pulled a string off the neck, and it grounded on the neck pick-up, giving me something like a high D. It sounded like I slid up to a super high note that isn't even on the neck, so we left it. For the next solo we used backwards guitar parts. To get them I played a bunch of guitar parts that were in the same key as the song and laid them down on quarter-inch tape. Then we flipped the tape over and edited it, so we had two or three minutes of backwards guitar. We put it in the last verse of the song.

HETFIELD: I think we wanted to write another song like "Creeping Death," with open chords carried by the vocals and a real catchy chorus. On *Master of Puppets* we started getting into the longer, more orchestrated songs. It was more of a challenge to write a long song that didn't seem long. The riff for that song was pretty messy—constantly moving. It works good live; people love to scream "Master!" a couple of times.

"WELCOME HOME (Sanitarium)" *(Master of Puppets, 1986)*

HAMMETT: The beginning of the first solo is an arpeggiated ninth chord figure, where I basically mirror what James is playing. The second guitar figure had some harmonies. I used a wah-wah pedal on the third solo, which was pretty straight ahead. The fourth solo comes out of harmonized guitars; the very last lick was based on something really cool I saw Cliff play on guitar in the hotel one night that I knew would work in that spot.

HETFIELD: The idea for that song came from the movie *One Flew Over the Cuckoo's Nest.* "Fade to Black" worked well, and we wanted to have another slow, clean, picking type of song, this time with a chorus. I had trouble singing that chorus. It's really high, and when I went to sing it in the studio, I remember Flemming looking at me like, "You're kidding." I said "Shit, I don't know if I can do this!" So I ended up singing it lower than I intended, but we put a higher harmony on it and it worked pretty well. The riff for that song was lifted from some other band, who shall remain anonymous.

The $5.98 EP/GARAGE DAYS RE-REVISITED (1987)

HAMMETT: That was recorded when I first started using ESP guitars with EMG pickups. All the lead guitar parts on that EP flowed really quickly; I did them in two nights. All of the leads were mine. The fact that the original versions of "Helpless" and "The Wait" don't even have solos in them was a bit of luck—no one would have anything to compare them to, and it kept any preconceived ideas out of my head. We did that EP for the fans, just for fun, and Elektra loved it and released it. Though it recently went Platinum, we feel it served its purpose, and it's since been deleted.

HETFIELD: Putting out an EP of all cover tunes was absolutely unheard of, which we thought was really cool. We didn't do too many arrangements, except to some of the Budgie tunes, where we eliminated some lame singing parts. For some of the songs we tuned down to D to make them a little heavier. The guitar sound is really awful, but it was the first thing we put out where the bass could be heard, so Jason [*Newsted, bassist*] was happy.

"ONE"(*...And Justice for All*, 1988)

HAMMETT: I used a Mesa-Boogie power-amp, an '88 preamp and an Aphex parametric EQ on this album. We wanted a clean guitar sound for "One." The first solo went fine, but I had trouble with the second; I just couldn't nail it. I only had eight days to record all my leads because we were heading out on the Monsters of Rock tour. As a result, I was never happy with what was on the record, and I flew to the Hit Factory in New York between gigs to patch up the solos. I did the third solo in a couple of hours. I worked out the first right-hand tapping thing, and from there it flowed very well. I think it worked because I was so pissed off that the second solo wasn't working out. When I had to play that live, it didn't feel right because it was so clean. So I started playing it full volume with full distortion on my neck pickup, and liked it better. In retrospect, I think I should have played it that way on the album.

HETFIELD: I had been fiddling around with that A-G modulation for a long time. The idea for the opening came from a Venom song called "Buried Alive." The kick drum machine-gun part near the end wasn't written with the war lyrics in mind, it just came out that way. We started that album with Mike Clink as producer. He didn't work out too well, so we got Flemming to come over and save our asses.

"...AND JUSTICE FOR ALL" (*...And Justice for All*, 1988)

HAMMETT: I worked out an opening lick for the solo but it wasn't really happening, so I plugged in the wah-wah pedal—which I always do when all else fails. As soon as I plugged in, we were done. A lot of people give me shit about how I hide behind the wah pedal, but something about it brings out a lot of aggression. It just tailors the sound to match the mood and emotion I'm trying to convey. It's purely an aesthetic thing and not a crutch or anything like that. The riff where I utilize the open string hammer-ons developed from a Gary Moore lick that I'd been studying. I figured it would sound really good combined with the heavy E-chord progression.

HETFIELD: That song is pretty long, like all the songs on that album. We wanted to write shorter material, but it never happened. We were into packing songs with riffs. The whole riff is very percussive; it goes right along with the drums. The singing on that song is a lot lower than usual.

"DON'T TREAD ON ME" (*Metallica*, 1991)

HAMMETT: I used a Bradshaw because the mids were clean and the low end sounded real percussive. The harmonic distortion also sounded nice and dirty. For the highs we used two Marshalls. We combined all the sounds and put the Bradshaw preamp through a VHT power-amp. We put it all through Marshall cabinets with 30-watt speakers and blended all the room mikes. My sound is a lot thicker and punchier than before, and I think it's better than ever. For the majority of the leads on this album I used a third ESP guitar. I also used my 1989 black Gibson Les Paul Custom. For the clean sound, I used a '61 stock white Strat and a Fender black-face Deluxe. I also used a '53 Gibson ES-295 style, and an ESP Les Paul Junior with EMG pickups.

I used the '89 black Gibson Les Paul Custom and a wah-wah pedal on "Don't Tread on Me." At one point I had to play these ascending lead fills, and it just wasn't happening at all. So I wound up playing harmonics instead of lead guitar fills, and it worked really well.

HETFIELD: A lot of the songs on this album are more simple and concentrated. They tell the same story as our other shit but don't take as long. There aren't a hundred riffs to latch on to—just two or three stock, really good riffs in each song.

I used my ESPs and tons of other guitars: a 12-string electric, a Telecaster, a Gretsch White Falcon, a sitar and other things. I also used a B-Bender—a bar installed in the guitar that twists the B string up a full step. It's used a lot in country music. But "Don't Tread" is just real heavy guitar—there's really nothing else to it.

"THE GOD THAT FAILED" *(Metallica*, 1991)

HAMMETT: I had this whole thing worked out, but it didn't fit because the lead was too bluesy for the song, which is characterized by real heavy riffing and chording. So producer Bob Rock and I worked out a melody, to which I suggested that we add a harmony part. But Bob said it would only pretty it up. So we ended up playing the melody an octave higher, and it sounded great. We basically mapped out the whole solo, picking the best parts from about 15 solos I'd worked out. It's one of my favorite solos on the album.

One thing I did on this album that I hadn't done before was play guitar fills. I filled up holes—like when James stops during the vocal, I put in a little stab or, as Bob calls it, a "sting." My solos on this album are a little offbeat. Though a lot of guitar players start the solo on the downbeat—the first beat of the measure—I come in on the upbeat of the third measure of a bar, like on "Enter Sandman" and "Don't Tread on Me."

HETFIELD: That's a very nice song. Slow, heavy and ugly. There are a lot of single-note riffs and more open-chord shit on this album. A lot of the rhythms I came up with were a little too complicated— half-step changes and other weirdo shit that Kirk had trouble soloing over. So we simplified some things. All the harmony guitar stuff on this album is incorporated in the rhythm tracks. I played rhythm all the way through, then I overdubbed harmony guitar things. There are harmony solos and harmony guitar in the rhythms, but they're very distinct from each other. We found that layering a guitar six times doesn't make it heavy.

Neil Zlozower

GUITAR WORLD, NOVEMBER 1988

METAL MILITIA

Kirk Hammett and Metallica take America by storm on the Monsters of Rock tour and with the monster album ...AND JUSTICE FOR ALL.

By Jeff Spurrier

O ANY METALLICA maniac, the chain of events that transpired during the band's set at the L.A. Coliseum Monsters of Rock show was about as predictable as the clichéd ham-fisted riffs churned out by the other acts on the bill. During Metallica's third song, an estimated 15,000 fans breached the wire barricades set up around the floor of the arena. Under a blistering mid-afternoon sun, the metal militia battered down a fence and rushed the stage in a lemming-like onslaught that left the yellow-jacketed security guards running for cover. "AlcoholicA," read one of the banners unfurled among the mass of bodies. "Drink 'Em All," read another, a pun on the band's debut album, *Kill 'Em All*, as well as the group's dipsomaniac reputation.

Throughout Metallica's performance, objects rained in from the crowd: shoes, hats, plastic spritzer bottles, shirts. At one point, drummer Lars Ulrich leaned over his drum riser at the rear of the stage and made a one-handed catch of a thong sandal heading his way. He held it up like a trophy, grinned devilishly and gave a thumbs-up sign before throwing it back.

As the band played on, the frenzy of the audience shifted into overdrive, and soon the plastic chairs used for seating on the arena floor were being passed over heads toward the stage. Pieces of the chairs came flying in with the shoes and hats until finally a whole chair was thrown, nearly hitting singer James Hetfield. At that moment, the PA system conveniently gave out and the band quickly retired to the backstage area while efforts were made to defuse the near-riot mood.

After the band left the stage, thousands streamed out of the stadium, many stopping to buy $18 Metallica T-shirts from the concession stands. And although it was still early—Dokken, the Scorpions and Van Halen were still to come—some of the fans didn't bother to stick around.

"Metallica is why I came," said one 20-year-old Long Beacher. "I don't even know if I'm going to go back in. They kicked ass! They don't have copped-out attitudes. Their music is so perfect, and they're not a bunch of assholes. They've mastered what they do. They're speed metal, but they have melodic things in there too, which you don't see from a lot of speed metal bands. Usually it's just straight-out thrash. There's nobody to compare Kirk Hammett to— except maybe Randy Rhoads."

If you had to pick someone to inherit the mantle of fallen metal legend Randy Rhoads, you couldn't find a more unlikely candidate than 25-year-old Kirk Hammett. But then, there's little about Metallica that fits neatly preconceived notions. Although Metallica is one of the leading proponents of speed metal, the band has distinguished itself from its peers with complex song structures, issue-oriented lyrics, long songs that defy handy radio formatting and an appreciation for melody even within the over-amped environment of metal, a genre not known for subtlety. With their reliance upon word-of-mouth popularity and a casual, down-to-earth style, the band has become a true grass roots phenomenon. Based on the wild enthusiasm evident at the Monsters shows, critics are already predicting that the band's next album, ...And Justice for All, will hit Number One.

The key, says Hammett, is originality. "We've gotten as far as we have because we offer something different," he says. "There were bands like Motorhead and Diamond Head doing this before us; we were just at the right place at the right time. There are a lot of thrash metal bands that wouldn't even think of doing a ballad. We've had a ballad on every album since *Ride the Lightning* (1984). We're not afraid to try different things, like slowing down arrangements or not screaming all the time or singing real melodies. Even on the leads I play, I try to be as different as possible. Everyone now is trying to do this Yngwie thing—playing at ten thousand miles an hour—and everyone does it better than I do, so I don't even bother."

In a hotel room the day after the L.A. Coliseum show, Hammett sits back on the sofa and props his legs up on a coffee table. With his hair pulled back, his glasses on and a soft whisper of a mustache, he looks much younger than his actual age, 25. Somewhat shy and self-effacing, Hammett offstage doesn't come across like one might expect one of speed metal's leading lights to. While his performance the day before was red-hot, with arpeggios and three-octave scales ripped off with casual aplomb, in person he seems guilelessly insecure, readily acknowledging his ongoing struggle to blend technical expertise with the band's herky-jerky tempos and convoluted song structure. There's no posturing, no canned answers, no self-aggrandizement. In fact, one of the first things he says is that the spotlight on him should be broadened to include rhythm guitarist James Hetfield.

Hammett started playing guitar 10 years ago, as a teenager in the small San Francisco Bay-area town of El Sobrante. Like fledgling players everywhere, he spent years trying to find the right combination of components that would give him the perfect sound. His first rig, "a piece-of-shit Montgomery Ward's catalog electric guitar and a cardboard shoe-box amp with a four-inch speaker," was abandoned after a few weeks. He borrowed a neighbor's Stella, played it for a few years and then got his first real guitar, a 1978 Strat.

"I could never get a full sound out of it," he recalls, "mostly because I was playing through shit amps. I did a lot of experimenting with it, putting in different pickups. I tried DiMarzios, Bill Lawrence humbuckers and some others. I never knew that full sound

I heard on records was coming through beefed-up Marshalls. Later, I managed to get hold of a Randall bass amp, but I still wasn't successful. Then I got a Sunn amp with C-MOS technology and solid-state distortion, and that was it—I finally had that overdriven, distorted sound. I traded in my Strat, and for 200 dollars more I got a '74 Gibson Flying V. I had just discovered Michael Schenker and thought he was great."

With his Flying V (which he still frequently uses on record) and Sunn amp, Hammett started playing in bands, only to face a new problem. The sound became too distorted. After a stint at Burger King, he earned enough money to buy a Marshall half-stack and finally found the right mix.

Metallica recruited him to join just before the band was getting ready to record their first album, 1983's *Kill 'Em All.* "I played my first gig with them a week later on the East Coast, and actually, they never told me I was in the band," he laughs. "After we were in the studio making the album, I figured I was in."

Around the same time, Hammett met up with the person who would drastically alter his approach to the guitar: Berkeley guitar teacher Joe Satriani.

"In 1982 and 1983, the heavy metal scene in San Francisco was really healthy and fruitful. There were a lot of bands and a lot of competition amongs guitar players. I found out then that there were two types of [metal] guitar players: your basic Eddie Van Halen clone and your stylized heavy metal player. I didn't want to become a Van Halen clone. And there was this one guitar player [on the club circuit] whose style I really liked. He was doing arpeggios and three-octave solos, so I asked him where he learned his stuff. He told me about Joe, so I called him and started taking lessons from him. I took about 20 lessons over five years."

For the first time, Hammett was learning how and why certain metal guitarists chose certain scales and riffs. Satriani explained why some licks worked and why others didn't. "Eventually," Hammett recalls, "I stopped bringing him stuff to show me, and we just concentrated on theory. We studied chord chemistry, modes, how to build scales off of different degrees and chord progressions. [*The results of the lessons*] became really apparent in 1984 and 1985. That was when my whole style really changed. He showed me how to harmonize with the band. And I've been applying what I learned from Joe over the last four years. After a while, the band couldn't tell what was influenced by Joe and what wasn't."

Satriani isn't the only guitarist Hammett cites as inspirational; Jimi Hendrix, Ulrich Roth and Michael Schenker all are on his list of influences. In fact, he says, he admires just about anybody who plays "a really good guitar solo."

And what's that?

"Something that's melodic, intense, aggressive and has hooks in it," he says. "Someone like George Lynch. He has a really bluesy feel in the middle of all these pyrotechnics. He'll do these wild hammer-ons and sweep arpeggios and then go into something really melodic that harmonizes. Gary Moore can also be really melodic and intense at the same time. And Steve Vai. He has a huge sense of humor in his playing, like he's cracking jokes with his guitar. And Joe—he has a lot of melody and he's really catchy and dynamic. That's so important. It's like the old saying of trying to tell a story with your guitar. It's a cliché, but it's true."

Even after his years of study with Satriani, Hammett admits that he's still not totally confident with his technique. When he's off the road, he plays constantly—immediately after waking up, during the afternoon, watching TV at night—and captures anything he likes on a Fostex four-track.

Hammett always begins these workouts with exercises. "Scales, arpeggios, chromatic exercises—although I have trouble memorizing scales," he admits. "Especially three-octave modes. They're the hardest to memorize when you play them in cycles of fourths. Before we go on stage, I'll go through my modes in cycles of fourths and jam on parts of songs, trying to come up with something new. I practice scales every day— at least until I feel warmed up."

No amount of warming up eased the pressure the band felt going in to record their latest release. During the ...*And Justice for All* sessions, Metallica was getting ready for the Monsters of Rock tour, and rather than enjoying his usual relaxed schedule to polish his solos, Hammett found himself working long hours trying to make things work.

"From a technical point of view, this album was a nightmare," he grimaces. "There were so many tempo changes. James would come up with a rhythm background, and the only scale that would fit would be a minor pentatonic scale with a flatted fifth. Trying to be melodic in an altered scale like that was a nightmare. In 'Blackened,' there are four different tempo and rhythm background changes, and for me to make it smooth all the way through was really challenging. To this day, I don't think I did it successfully. People tell me differently, but in my head I know otherwise.

"There's something about being in the studio, in the heat of the moment when the red light goes on, that just makes you want to change things around," he continues. "After playing to rehearsal tapes for three months where it's slightly out-of-tempo and the recording isn't the best, suddenly you're in there hearing perfect drum tracks, perfect guitar tracks—everything is picture-perfect—it really bothers me. I did all my leads for the album in seven days because I had to. The Monsters tour was coming up. When you do stuff that quickly, you settle for something, and when you go back and listen to it, you may discover it's not happening. Things sound forced. I was working 16 hours a day doing solos, and when you work that long, you start to lose your perspective. Your ear goes down the drain."

There was one aspect to the *Justice* recording that was not a nightmare for Hammett: getting the tone he wanted from his guitar. Unlike the *Master of Puppets* session, when he spent three days in the studio trying to get the right sound, this time the tone came a little easier.

"I knew what I wanted," he says. "During *Master* I wasn't 100 percent sure. There's nothing more discouraging than working on something for eight hours and at the end of the session knowing it's crap. I think the guitar tones on this album are some of the better lead tones I've gotten. The rhythm sound that James got is amazing. We didn't have time to do anything super-weird, which I wanted to do. I wanted to experiment a lot more."

The *Justice* recording sharply contrasts *The $5.98 EP/Garage Days Re-Revisited*, the band's 1987 five-song compilation of British heavy metal and punk covers. The EP was released following a pair of nearly devastating incidents: the death of original bassist Cliff Burton in a bus accident in Sweden, and a skateboarding injury that left Hetfield with a broken arm. The imposed hiatus found the band going back to their roots in a converted garage in Oakland, jamming on old Misfits and Diamond Head songs. The EP was recorded in six days with little concern for mistakes, bad notes or feedback. It's certainly not one of the best-recorded metal albums, but it is immediately seductive for its charm and youthful naiveté. It feels like an extension of one of the band's off-time country jams when they get together with their friends in the Bay area, retreat to a ranch outside the city and play wild garage tribal thrash long into the night.

Comparing *Garage Days* to *...And Justice for All* is like watching a time-lapsed film of a plant emerging from a seed. There's maturity, sophistication and a sense of direction present in songs like "Blackened," "One" and "Dyer's Eve" that should propel Metallica out of their cult status into genuine hard-rock mainstream popularity. Despite speed metal's teenage aura, Metallica is clearly not just for the angst-and-acne set. The attitude that emerges from their lyrics, personal style and musical technique shows that this is a band that refuses to play down—either to themselves or their audience.

"I'm not into that whole Satanic thing," says Hammett, obviously embarrassed by the blood, guts and Satanic symbols employed by some metal bands. "It's something to fall back on if you don't have much imagination. Singing your 50th song about having lunch with Satan—I'm not into it. It's silly. I see people out there trying to be so macho and heavy, and I think, 'You've got to be kidding. You can't actually try to push this on an audience and expect them to believe it.' But people get away with it. I feel if you can't take the band seriously, then you can't take the music seriously. For a group like that to sing about the crisis in Central America…Come on, it would never work."

On the other hand, Metallica's lyrics—penned by Hetfield—do work. Their themes of nuclear destruction, censorship and McCarthyism are frequently bleak and the images graphically stark, but it's obvious that it's not just for shock value. The band insists on having a lyric sheet on the inner sleeve of its albums so that its audience gets the message.

"With heavy music you should have heavy lyrics," Hammett says. "Not just, 'Hey baby, let's drink a lot and puke on each other all night!' 'One' is one of my favorite songs on …*And Justice for All*. I thought we captured the entire mood and the chain of events told in the book."

The book Hammett is referring to is not some gothic thriller by H.P. Lovecraft, but rather Dalton Trumbo's classic anti-war story, *Johnny Got His Gun*. Closer to home, the song "The Shortest Straw" is about McCarthyism and blacklisting, a subject that Metallica has personal experience with after being placed on the PMRC's hit list.

"Something like [*McCarthyism*] almost happened with the PMRC," says Hammett. "If Tipper Gore's husband [*Al Gore*] hadn't been running for president, I think it would have gotten a lot worse. They had a picture of us in her book, and the caption was, 'This band promotes alcohol.' It was pretty funny, actually."

As Hammett speaks, MTV flickers from a silent TV nearby, and he stares blankly at the sight of a popular glam band prancing around the stage, all flash and makeup.

"For a band that doesn't play very well, they sure do have a lot of guitars," he mutters.

Like his bandmates, Kirk Hammett doesn't believe in setting himself up on a pedestal, removed from the fans. Their following has been built by word of mouth, not hype or MTV or radio play. There was some discussion before *Justice* was completed about recording shorter songs—the shortest song on *Master of Puppets* is over five minutes, while others are over eight minutes long—but the ultimate decision was to go with what they like. Demographically, says Hammett, "People who listen to the radio probably aren't our type of crowd."

Similarly, jumping on bandwagons or following trends is simply not the Metallica way. After some persistent probing, Hammett admits that he does have some classical influences, but he doesn't like talking about them.

"Everyone says, 'Oh, I'm a heavy metal guitarist, but I'm classically influenced,' " he groans. "It's so trendy that I hate to talk about it. But one of my favorite all-time albums is Christopher's *Parkening Plays Bach*. I love that. I went to see him with some friends seven months ago, and he was brilliant."

But is Kirk Hammett as brilliant in his chosen field? It's hard to say just yet. There's no doubt that the technical prowess is there; but as he himself concludes, that's not all there is to it.

"It's weird," he says, somewhat wearily. "I've found that, with all this study of technique, when you get right down to it, you throw all that out the window and go with what works best. I believe you have to have technique, but it's also good to detach yourself from all of it and go with what feels good. Just because you know umpteen billion scales, it doesn't mean you have to use them all in a solo."

It's just such an awareness that filters out the technicians from the artists, and Kirk Hammett seems to have the humility and love of his instrument to propel him into genuine superstardom. He's only 25, so who knows?

GUITAR WORLD, OCTOBER 1991

DAMAGE INC.

Metallica's James Hetfield and Kirk Hammett beef up their tone, sharpen their attack and slash their thrash on METALLICA, the band's brutal new release.

By Jeff Gilbert

"WE'VE BEEN IN the studio so long, a war has come and gone, and we're still stuck in here!" A heavy weariness, quite evident behind James Hetfield's steely gaze, underscores the intense pressure that has been Metallica's constant companion over the past few months as they've labored to record *Metallica*, their first album in more than three years, and fifth overall. "It's pretty amazing when you think about it," offers Hetfield with a strained smile.

Here within the comfortable confines of One on One Studios in North Hollywood, it's down to the 11th hour for the world's greatest metal band. Working exhaustively around the clock with producer Bob Rock, Hetfield and Kirk Hammett take turns spit-polishing a guitar solo here, roughing out a vocal there. While this modern recording facility is outfitted with pool tables, weights, a well-stocked kitchen, dart boards, big screen TVs, exercise machines and just about any creature-comfort a healthy (or otherwise) rock group could ever want, it has been a veritable Devil's Island for Metallica.

"We've seen four other bands come through and do their albums," growls Hetfield. "And some of those guys have already gone on tour!"

Outside, a small group of roving Metallica fans, hoping to catch a glimpse of James or Kirk entering (but never, seemingly, leaving) the white, windowless stucco building, maintains a tireless vigil, shuffling up and down the 5200 block of Lankershim Boulevard. Their nervous, darting eyes and untucked Metallica shirts have some local business proprietors double-checking their wares and wallets.

"This has been going on since last October, once them kids found out this heavy metal band was next door," says a leathery-looking taco vendor a block away. "They don't scare me none, though." As if on cue, a few scruffy fans wander in and order some burritos, heavy on the grease.

Inside the studio, Bob Rock is screaming. His voice penetrates the bank-vault thickness of the studio doors, almost reaching the street outside. The producer is at the hair-pulling stage after spending the past five and a half hours trying to correct a single, renegade guitar note that, to his million-dollar ears, is a microscopic tone out of whack. "He's not having a good day," Hammett suggests with a sheepish grin. The guitarist is repeatedly called in to try to punch in a note that will allow the visibly stressed Canadian producer to finally wrap up the tedious session. Kirk excuses himself, runs into the studio's main room, shoulders a black ESP and effortlessly runs through the solo for the 20th time. "I think I got it," he says.

It's no small wonder that Bob Rock—the career-rescuing hit-maker for artists like Motley Crue, Aerosmith, the Cult and Bon Jovi—is concerned with something as seemingly trivial as a single guitar note. Taking on the Metallica project was a critical step in his otherwise Top 40-oriented career. "People will be saying Bob made Metallica sound like Bon Jovi," remarks James. "They don't realize that no one screws with us, except us. Bob fit right into the program and the direction we were going."

Certainly, Rock's commercially successful background has raised more than a few eyebrows among Metallica's many supporters. The notion of Hetfield and company opting for the producer's trademark approach—crisp, clear guitars and radio-friendly hooks—is enough to severely traumatize fans who drink in sledgehammer chords like they're mother's milk.

"We're not really out to justify what we're doing," says Hetfield defensively. "We don't give a shit. This is what we want and this is how it is. Bob just helped us get what we want."

What they wanted for *Metallica*, and what they got, were guitars that ring more sharply than ever, leaving a clean trail of resonating destruction. Where ...*And Justice for All* was weak and flat sounding in the bass and drum mix, the new album bursts with a deep snare crack and a bass thick and heavy enough to set cement with. The band's whiplash tempo changes and complicated arrangements have been revamped into a lethal and immensely heavy, groove-laden sound and album that should give thrash a sharp kick in its sluggish ass.

"Kirk!" Rock's screams are getting louder.

"Uh, oh," says Hammett, jumping up like a dog about to be punished for knocking over the garbage can. "Got to go."

GUITAR WORLD: Your patented "Metalli-crunch" seems bigger and badder than ever on the new album. What did you do to fatten your sound?

KIRK HAMMETT: First, I went through my CD collection and picked out guitar sounds that impressed me, and gave them to Bob Rock as points of reference. It helps to know what kind of tone you're trying to pursue.

GW: What discs did you give him?

HAMMETT: I was particularly impressed with Gary Moore's sound on his latest album, *Still Got the Blues*. I used one of the breaks from "Oh, Pretty Woman" as a main reference. I also gave Bob UFO's *Obsession*—I've always liked Michael Schenker's sound. The third example was something by Carlos Santana. I was shooting for a real up-front sounding guitar.

GW: But wasn't that the problem with ...*And Justice for All*? The guitar was so up-front that it obscured Jason's [Newsted] bass.

JAMES HETFIELD: The bass was obscured for two reasons. First, on past albums, Jason tended to double my rhythm guitar parts, so it was hard to tell where my guitar started and his bass left off. Also, my tone on *Justice* was very scooped—all lows and highs with very little mid-range. When my rhythm parts were placed in the mix, my guitar sound ate up all the lower frequencies. Jason and I were always battling for the same space in the mix.

On this album, Jason approached his parts differently. He's playing more with Lars' kick drum, so his bass lines are very distinct from my guitar lines—we're not getting in each other's way. Bob really helped us with orchestrating and bringing out the low end—getting the guitar and bass to work together. In fact, when I played the album for a friend, he asked, "What is that weird low-end sound?" I said, "That's something new for us—it's called bass!"

GW: Did Bob understand the Metallica guitar sound?

HETFIELD: Oh yeah, and he actually added to it. After we recorded some of the new album, we pulled out the actual master tapes from *Justice* and singled out the guitar sound. I discovered something that I already knew—that my *Justice* sound lacked body. As I mentioned earlier, mid-range has always been a no-no for me, but Bob showed me that having a touch of it in there really adds to your tone.

I think he was a little intimidated at the start because he wasn't sure how far he could push us. Bob was trying to be real professional, so we had to loosen him up. He was really polite at first, and would say things like, "It's your album, do whatever you want," and "It's only my opinion, but how about if we try this?" [*laughs*] However, seven months in the studio with Metallica tends to change a man. And Bob's been changed. [*laughs*] He's got a few more gray hairs, a few more wrinkles, he grew a tumor and has some sore knuckles from hitting the studio walls.

HAMMETT: Yeah, he really loosened up. In no time he was screaming and yelling and saying stuff like, "You have to get angry for this part—play it really mean and dirty!" Then we'd record another part, and he'd say, "Be bluesy and bendy." And to illustrate his point, Bob would move his shoulders all around. I'd just stare at him like he was a madman, thinking, "Uh, well, okay." But his approach eventually worked. I really started focusing on what he was trying to say. He encouraged me to think conceptually—not with my fingers. I thought a lot about what I felt would be the best way to approach the solo from a mental standpoint. As a result, my solos turned out smoother and more confidently executed.

GW: Were you ever afraid that Bob was going to turn Metallica into a pop band?

HETFIELD: Some people thought Bob would make us sound too commercial. You know, "Oh, Bob works with Bon Jovi; Bob works with Motley Crue." But if [*former Metallica producer*] Flemming Rasmussen worked on a Bon Jovi record, would Bon Jovi all of a sudden sound like Metallica? We chose Bob because we were really impressed with his crisp, full-sounding production on the Cult's *Electric* album and on Motley Crue's *Dr. Feelgood*.

HAMMETT: We wanted to create a different record and offer something new to our audience. I hate it when bands stop taking chances. A lot of bands put out the same record three or four times, and we didn't want to fall into that rut.

The truth is, we may have been guilty in the past of putting out the same running order—you know, start out with a fast song, then the title track, then a ballad. Other than that, though, we've really tried to create something different every time we went into the studio. And on *Metallica*, we made a conscious effort to alter and expand the band's basic elements.

GW: Did you experiment with different amps and cabinets?

HETFIELD: We tried a bunch of amps, but I ended up using the same Mesa/Boogie Simul-class Mark II that I've used on the last three albums. In Los Angeles there are a million amps you can try out, but none of them were up to snuff. Bob also brought in a bunch of crappy-looking vintage amps. We gave everything a shot and ended up with the same old shit. [*laughs*]

I must admit, though, it was a lot of fun trying out all those little Sixties and Seventies amps—they really sounded unique. A lot of metal players have forgotten that they can be useful. We used a couple of vintage amps for texture. But I wasn't about to play a rhythm part through a fucking Fender Supro amp, you know? We sure as hell weren't making *Led Zeppelin I*.

GW: Kirk, what did you use for amplification?

HAMMETT: I used a Bradshaw preamp for the lows and mids, and a couple of Marshalls for the nice clean highs. We EQ'd it through the board a little bit, and it worked out great.

The miking process was pretty simple. Bob had an engineer move a mic around in front of the cabinet until I heard the sound I wanted.

GW: Is your studio setup the same as your live setup?

HETFIELD: My live sound doesn't work in the studio, which is a completely different animal. Every little thing is detrimental to the sound. And if someone moves a mic, you've lost it. It's pretty much a case of "lock the door and set up a police line."

GW: What do you look for in an amp?

HETFIELD: A smooth, solid, round sound. Something that doesn't sound fake. You can always fiddle around with the EQ later. A lot of modern amps and preamps sound great when you're jamming by yourself, but they don't hold up in a band situation. The sound isn't dense enough, and the lows and highs tend to get soaked up by the bass and cymbals.

GW: James, you also tried a variety of guitars, which seems a little out of character for you.

HETFIELD: My primary guitar was an ESP Explorer with EMG pickups, but I also used a Telecaster, a Gretsch White Falcon with a Bigsby and a Guild 12-string. I used the other guitars just for bits and pieces.

GW: Kirk, I understand you didn't use your '74 Gibson Flying V on this record. What was your primary axe?

HAMMETT: I used two guitars—a Strat-style ESP with two EMGs and an '89 Gibson Les Paul Deluxe with two EMGs. The way I settled on those guitars is pretty funny. At the beginning of the recording process, I laid down one of my solos 15 times, using 15 different guitars. Then I listened to each track and—without knowing which guitar was which—selected the tone that sounded the best. I finally narrowed it down to the ESP and the Les Paul.

GW: And you nailed the solo perfectly each time?

HAMMETT: Well, not exactly. [*laughs*] Good enough to A-B them, though. It was kind of interesting to play all those different guitars. Bob brought in a lot of different guitars, too. He's a guitar player— or so he says. [*laughs*]

GW: What happened to your black '74 Gibson Flying V?

HAMMETT: I used that V on every album prior to this one, but the ESP just sounded a bit rounder. Also, I felt it was time for a change. I bought that V while working at a Burger King. I worked three months, just long enough to be able to afford it. As soon as I made $400—enough money to buy the V—I quit. I don't even know how much it costs to buy a guitar these days—I haven't set foot in a guitar store in ages.

GW: The songs on the new album are shorter than usual.

HETFIELD: Metallica shorter—six minutes instead of 10.

GW: It should be easier to get some radio airplay.

HETFIELD: That was always a problem. We'd record a song that people liked and wanted to hear on the radio, and the radio bastards wouldn't play it because it was too long. Or they would want to edit it, which we wouldn't allow.

But radio airplay wasn't the whole idea behind us writing shorter songs. It just seemed to us that we had pretty much done the longer song format to death. We were only able to fit about 12 songs in a two-and-a-half hour show. These shorter songs are going to help a bit—we're going to be able to play more of 'em. [*laughs*] We have one song that has just two riffs in it, which is pretty amazing. It only takes two minutes to get the point across!

GW: Shorter songs mean shorter guitar solos.

HAMMETT: In some instances.

GW: Also, the new album is less complex, harmonically.

HAMMETT: That's true. There are fewer key changes. There aren't many flatted fourth progressions or anything like that—just straight-ahead major and minor keys. The most complex song is probably

"Anywhere I Roam," which suggests a Phrygian dominant scale.

GW: Metallica has acquired a reputation for being meticulous in the studio. How often do you go back and repair something you think could be improved?

HAMMETT: I fix things all the time. Every time I do a solo, I recheck it and correct things that don't hit the mark.

GW: In doing so, do you ever get the feeling that your behavior is less musical than it is…anal retentive?

HAMMETT: [*laughs*] It's like this—you have to live with it. When you know you're going to be listening to a performance over 500 times, it's important to be happy with it. Believe me, there are mistakes on our other albums, and I can't bring myself to listen to them. It's torture.

GW: Which cuts?

HAMMETT: I'm not going to say! [*laughs*] You have to pick them out yourself.

GW: What really stands out about *Metallica* is its feel.

HETFIELD: That's what we wanted—a live feel. In the past, Lars and I constructed the rhythm parts without Kirk and Jason, or Lars played to a click by himself. This time I wanted to try playing as a band unit in the studio. It lightens things up, and you get more of a vibe. Everyone was in the same room and we were able to watch each other. That helped a lot, especially with some of the bass and lead stuff. It also helped that we'd played most of the songs for two months before we entered the studio.

Unfortunately, Lars kind of pussied out at the end—he didn't want everyone there. I guess it's kind of difficult to work in the studio when you're not used to a new song and there are all these people around.

GW: Lars is always very involved in the Metallica production process. What is his input with regard to the guitar sound?

HETFIELD: He doesn't mess with the guitar sound—just the bass guitar. [*laughs*] He can say whatever he wants, but I think he's pretty confident in my ability to know what's right as far as the guitar goes.

GW: While the songs on *Metallica* are less complex, the orchestration on this album is more sophisticated than your previous efforts.

HETFIELD: That's right. I think the degree of subtlety may shock people. Bob's really good with sound, and we took advantage of that by using different guitars and more vocal harmonies.

There are fewer guitar overdubs on this record, though. I used to layer 80 guitars in my attempt to create a heavy sound. While making this album, I discovered that sheer quantity doesn't necessarily make for a heavier sound; if anything, overdubs make guitars sound mushier. As far as rhythms go, there are either two or three tracks, and they're split pretty evenly. There is a lot more separation on this album, which also makes it sound punchier. With a pair of headphones, you can tell who's doing what.

GW: Were there any songs that didn't make it to the album?

HETFIELD: No. We went in and recorded 12. There are no other half-written songs sitting around anywhere. Whatever we wrote is there. It only takes one day of trying to write something to tell if it's going to end up in the dumper. [*laughs*]

GW: Kirk, "The Unforgiven" features an unusual solo. How did it evolve?

HAMMETT: That was probably the most challenging solo on the album. I had something worked out before I got into the studio, but Bob felt it wasn't quite appropriate. He asked if I could try something dirtier and more sustaining—something more in the Jeff Beck vein. At first I was kind of hurt, but then I realized he was right. I started fingerpicking a chordal thing, and Bob liked the way it sounded. He said, "Why don't you play that entire guitar solo with your fingers, and really pull on the strings and slap them against the frets?" It was a cool idea. I did it, and it sounded really percussive. That was the first time I fingerpicked a guitar solo on an album.

GW: That's a great example of a song that was a challenge, feel-wise. Did anything challenge your harmonic capabilities?

HAMMETT: "Of Wolf and Man" reminded me of some of the more progressive music on *Justice*. The rhythm parts jumped from a I chord to a bV chord—from E to Bb—which always presents a problem. I was stumped at first, but after a while I just started singing various lines and adapting my vocal melodies for the guitar. I discovered that singing breaks down a lot of imaginary boundaries and disrupts that tendency to gravitate towards familiar scales and finger patterns on the guitar.

GW: Does the band offer much input regarding your guitar solos?

HAMMETT: Sometimes I need an objective opinion, and it's good to ask the guys. But you know, I'll only change so much. [*laughs*] They'll make suggestions, but they never tell me what to play. It's more like, "I'm going to play what I think feels good, and if you don't like it, you tell me, and maybe I'll change it." We had a really big argument about a certain guitar solo. I said, "No, this is the way I want it to turn out." And that's the way we kept it. But it's good to have an objective opinion around, because it can lead to other areas and directions you didn't consider in the first place.

GW: For example?

HAMMETT: The solo that really comes to mind is the one in "The God That Failed." I had this whole thing worked out, and Bob said, "I don't know if that's going to make it—try something like this." And he half sang, half mumbled something. The only things really audible were the first three out of the eight or nine notes he was trying to sing. So I took those three notes and came up with a phrase that actually worked very well. Between his singing and my interpretation, we mapped out a solo that was a lot different from my original idea.

GW: James, why is it that you don't play any solos?

HETFIELD: I can't play leads. I can do really cool harmony shit, and on slow songs I can do bendy, feely-type shit, but my strength is in writing riffs. I just have a better feel for rhythm. I'll never be able to play fast like Kirk. I don't even try, because he's the man. He's using a lot of wah-wah lately, which everyone in the band really loves.

GW: Kirk, your use of the wah-wah pedal has almost become your signature.

HAMMETT: There's something about a wah pedal that really gets my gut going. People will probably say, "He's just hiding behind the wah." But that isn't the case. It's just that those frequencies really bring out a lot of aggression in my approach. Much of my playing is rhythmic and choppy; I use a lot of double stops. The wah just accents all those stops and chops and brings out the rhythmic aspect that much more.

The only problem I've had with my Vox wah is its tendency to move around on the floor. So now it sits on a rubber mat that says in big letters, "Kirk's Wah-Wah Rug." [*laughs*]

GW: Your solos on this album seem much more fluid than those you played in the past. What's your secret?

HAMMETT: We toured for a year and a half before we recorded this album, and that really helped my playing a lot. I also started listening to different kinds of music, which helped broaden my perspective. For example, I've been experimenting with slide guitar.

I also discovered a new recording process that really works for me. On *Metallica*, I recorded six or seven different guitar solos for almost every song, took the best aspects of each solo, mapped out a master solo and made a composite. Then I learned how to play the composite solo, tightened it up and replayed it for the final version. The only bad thing about that process is that it led to a lot of arguments.

GW: Didn't being in the studio for so long drive you crazy?

HETFIELD: Yes, it did! [*laughs*] Very much so. I don't remember doing anything else; I don't remember not living in the studio. I'm itching for people to hear this album because I'm sick of hearing it myself. That's the ultimate feeling—when someone hears your shit and says, "That's good!" And I go, "I know, but it's good to hear you say it!"

Neil Zlozower

GUITAR WORLD, OCTOBER 1991

THE LIGHTNING ROD

Drummer, songwriter and thrash visionary Lars Ulrich coolly assesses his guitar-slinging partners in grind.

By Jeff Gilbert

BEHIND EVERY GREAT guitar player is a great drummer. A roadie is indispensable, but a solid drummer is money in the bank. Metallica marches to the beat of Lars Ulrich, who is not only a highly practiced and supremely innovative drummer, but an avowed, unflinchingly die-hard guitar enthusiast. Lars is extremely fond of what he classifies as the "European" approach—the bluesy, melodic riffing of Uli Roth, Michael Schenker and, especially, Ritchie Blackmore. Few Metallica followers would be surprised to learn that Lars is a loud, guiding voice in the band. No slightly sour tone escapes his discerning ear; no half-baked solo sneaks by. In short, Metallica does little that has not first been approved by the drummer.

Lars, who over the past eight years has played with some of the best musicians in metal, is as outspoken as he is influential.

"I'm always amused," he says, sounding distinctly unamused, "by what's written in these guitar magazines—this whole thing about who can play the fastest, who can play backwards, who can do this harmonic minor 19th, and all of that crap. What ever happened to feel and style? All this emphasis on speed and technical ability just annoys me."

LARS ON KIRK HAMMETT:

"I've been in the studio for every solo Kirk has recorded for Metallica since *Kill 'Em All*. When Kirk gets a little too 'G.I.T.-ish,' I go, 'Hang on a second!' " laughs Lars. "All that harmonic minor fifth stuff over an arpeggiated fourth is Russian to me. I just try and help him get the solos to have a lot of rhythmic and dynamic variations. I help bring things out of Kirk that are catchy and cool.

"On *Metallica* the songs aren't so busy, and Kirk's guitar playing fits in well when he plays with the laid-back drums. James and I tried to set things up that were easier for Kirk to solo over. Some of the things on *Justice* got a little out of hand. Then it was, 'Okay, Kirk, solo over this!' And it would be the most sideways, difficult thing. I think Metallica spent a couple of years trying to prove to everybody that we could really play.

"I remember the first time I heard Kirk. He had a feel that very few young players have—very rooted in European metal. It was really nice to hear an American guy who didn't play like Eddie Van Halen. Over the last couple of years, Kirk's been able to retain his own identity and not get caught up in that Yngwie/Vai wave. He can certainly do all that stuff in his sleep. But the thing I think is so cool about Kirk is that he retains his feel."

LARS ON JAMES HETFIELD:

"Until the last few years, James was really underrated as a guitar player. I don't think people know how difficult some of his stuff really is to play, and how much of an accomplished all-around guitarist James is. It isn't just that he has the fastest right hand around, but that he's so fast picking every note down.

"He can play anything; the guy can jam funk and even friggin' country. And now that James has been hanging out with [*producer*] Bob Rock, he's really starting to open up and get an idea of how much more there is to the guitar. He even bought a banjo a few months ago. Believe me, seeing James playing the banjo is quite a visual trip.

"What he does with his right hand doesn't interest me. But I have a really strong connection to what he does on the guitar neck. To put it another way, I play guitar through his left hand."

LARS ON JASON NEWSTED:

"This time around, Jason really laid his musical abilities on the shelf and did what was right for the song, more so than anybody else in the band. He's a great bass player, and he played some really simple, effective stuff. Early on, I tried to get Jason to pay more attention to my hi-hat than to James' right hand. Whatever James picked, Jason would automatically double—and those really fast picking things would sound very messy on the bass. It took us eight years to realize there were other options!

"Jason works a lot more with the drums now, which really makes the guitars stand out. People always ask where the bass is on *Justice*. Well, the bass is a mirror image of what James was doing— which, in effect, obscures Jason.

"The new album was awkward for Jason for the first couple of days. Bob Rock, James and I would sit there telling him to play eighth notes on top of this really busy riff. Once he got the hang of it, he felt comfortable doing the right thing for the whole rhythm foundation. And who gives a shit what *Bass Player* magazine thinks?"

LARS ON LARS ULRICH:

"Sure, I play the guitar a little. But to say that I play guitar would definitely be an overstatement," he laughs. "If I were a guitar player, I'd probably go for the black left-handed Strat with the white pickguard—like the one Ritchie Blackmore used on *Fireball* and *Machine Head*. I think those guitars look incredible! When he played that Strat, Blackmore would usually start 'Smoke on the Water' with some dweedly thing. He'd go off for about 30 or 60 seconds and then, all of a sudden, flick the pickup switch and go into the Riff of Life! It was a major fuckin' attitude."

GUITAR WORLD, OCTOBER 1991

BOTTOMS UP

Jason Newsted is feeling groove-y, thanks to a variety of exotic basses and a little help from his friends.

By Jeff Gilbert

OKAY, HOLD UP a copy of ...*And Justice for All*. Examine the back cover photo. Look at the expression on Jason Newsted's face. Talk about pain. Angst, maybe. Was Jason's stomach a bit sour? Was his bass strung a little tight? Nope. Newsted, no doubt, was in agony because his bass cannot be heard on *Justice*. Oh, he played on the hit album; it says so right on the sleeve. So what happened?

"I can't explain how much grief I dealt with—and still deal with—over that record," moans Newsted during a short break from filming the video for "Sad but True," the first single from *Metallica*. "I used to always duplicate guitar parts on the bass. That's what I did in my previous band, Flotsam & Jetsam. I always knew it was just a matter of bringing it to realization—playing an actual bass part."

Under producer Bob Rock's careful guidance, Metallica's unhappiest member rethought his approach to playing bass. "I'm very proud of how much it came back around," Newsted says. "I think the bass sound on the new album is definitely much weightier than it's been."

GUITAR WORLD: *Metallica* is a lot heavier than some of its predecessors. The bass has made a comeback.

JASON NEWSTED: I'd like to think so. [*laughs*] Bob Rock spent a lot of time figuring out what bass frequencies were going to work with the guitars. They cover so much space, we had to find some room for the bass to fit in and still allow the kick drum to break through. It took some time.

GW: Which of your basses did you use most on the album?

NEWSTED: A Spector, which worked out great.

GW: Did you use your Alembics at all?

NEWSTED: Yeah. I tried out about 25 different basses. I went through P-basses, old Thunderbirds, new Thunderbirds, Paul Reed Smiths...you name it. But the Spector was the one.

GW: Did you experiment with different pickups?

NEWSTED: Not really; we had a nice selection of pickup configurations. But we did try different strings and different amps. I ended up using a combination of three or four different amps. I used 18-inch SVRs for the low end, a Marshall guitar cabinet with a Trace Elliot for a mid/high clickey thing, and an old Ampeg SVT head and cabinet for the meat of the sound.

GW: You wouldn't think that getting a good bass sound would be so complicated.

NEWSTED: [*laughs*] I never realized what it entailed. It used to be quick because nobody gave it much consideration. But in Bob Rock I found someone who knew what he wanted and how to achieve it. I learned a lot by listening for what was needed in terms of actual bass sound. I learned to bring lots of mids up in my sound. I didn't do that before. I spent about three weeks recording my tracks.

GW: Did you use your new Hamer Mandocello 12-string bass?

NEWSTED: Yeah. I played it on some different little pieces. I'm into playing eight-string, too. I have a bunch of those old Hagstroms, which sound pretty cool. I also have a Hamer eight-string. I was always into the multi-string thing, so it wasn't that hard to adapt to 12. I use them sometimes to play rhythm parts.

GW: When you enter the studio, do you usually have all your bass parts worked out?

NEWSTED: Yes. I had the songs down pretty well this time, and I tried to create a real rhythm section rather than a one-dimensional sound. If it takes a few eighth notes instead of just whipping around all over the place and losing the weight, then so be it.

GW: Did it take long to adjust to altering your playing style?

NEWSTED: It took a second. [*laughs*] But I realized that that's how it's got to be, and how I should be doing it anyway. Kirk and James have a big enough guitar sound, and are good enough players, so that they cover all that stuff anyway. When it comes time for a solo, I can cut loose and skeedle around. Now it comes down to the music—making it a real rhythm section for once, and letting the guitars do their work. I'm glad the rest of the band could tell me that that's what was needed.

GW: I know you use a pick on just about everything, but did you fingerpick on the acoustic numbers?

NEWSTED: On a couple of the mellower songs, I do hit a few strings with my fingers—and on the 12-string, to lighten my attack in a couple of spots. But most of the time, I use a pick. That's how I'm comfortable.

GW: Is Bob Rock responsible for those well-placed bass slides and swells?

NEWSTED: Oh, yeah. He made a lot of suggestions about those types of things, and I tried them all. He could always see five or seven steps ahead of my playing. I've never seen anything like that.

GW: What kind of strings do you use?

NEWSTED: LaBella's, .128 to .45 on the five-string, and .105 to .45 on the regular.

GW: Your road basses appear to be customized.

NEWSTED: Yeah, I pick the wood and everything. I also design the pickup configuration. Alembic has built my last 10 basses from my specs. Even if I go for an already existing shape, I'll modify the body contour so my arm comes down comfortably for picking. I had them put LEDs on the side of the neck—different little things like that. I also have things coated in brass and gold.

GW: One doesn't usually associate Alembics with Metallica-style music. What attracted you to them?

NEWSTED: I always thought they were incredible. As soon as I could afford one, I tried it—and that was it. Their factory is in Santa Rosa, so I can always go there and deal with them face to face, right down to the guy who helps me choose the wood.

GW: What are you going to use on the road?

NEWSTED: My Alembic stereo bass, four Ampeg 300-watt heads and several old Ampeg SVT 8x10 cabinets.

GW: Why is the album called *Metallica*?

NEWSTED: We just decided to keep it simple. It took us a long time to think up that title. [*laughs*] I guess we could have called it "Five," or titled it after one of the songs. I don't know; you got any ideas?

Neil Zlozower

GUITAR WORLD, AUGUST 1992

IRON MEN

So sayeth the book of Nostradamus: "In the year of our Lord 1992, the Master of Reality will meet the Master of Puppets." Metallica's James Hetfield and Black Sabbath's Tony Iommi meet in fulfillment of the old fraud's prophecy.
By Brad Tolinski with Alan Paul

TONY IOMMI AND James Hetfield arrive for the Great Encounter decked out in black. No one seems particularly surprised by their matching color scheme, as it would be cause for concern if they didn't look like twin executioners. Black, after all, is the official color of heavy metal royalty, and these are the kings of kings.

Their similar attire notwithstanding, Iommi and Hetfield's demeanors contrast sharply. The dark-eyed Iommi, with his meticulously groomed mustache and refined English accent, has the dignified bearing of a British nobleman. The blond, gravel-voiced Hetfield has the dour, hard-bitten aspect of an urban street-fighting man. His gruff exterior, however, disintegrates in a puff of worshipful smoke as soon as he greets Black Sabbath's legendary guitarist.

"It's a pleasure to finally meet you, man," Hetfield says with genuine enthusiasm.

Iommi is quick to respond with a volley of compliments. "My son bought me your last album, and it's one of first recordings I've received in a long time that I can praise without reservation. I listen to it in my car all the time."

Hetfield beams at these unqualified words of approval from hard rock's original god of thunder. As the leader of Black Sabbath, Iommi pioneered an entire school of dense, ominous, highly amplified music, which eventually became known as heavy metal. Though many guitarists experimented with power chords and distorted tones in the psychedelic Sixties, Iommi was the first to turn these elements into a personal obsession.

The original Sabbath line-up—Iommi, singer Ozzy Osbourne, bassist Geezer Butler and drummer Bill Ward—first coalesced in 1968 as Earth, playing pop and blues. One year later, the group discovered volume, overdrive and paranoia, and celebrated their find by adopting the sinister Sabbath moniker. Shortly thereafter, the band released *Black Sabbath*, the first of its series of hell-raising masterpieces on Warner Bros. *Paranoid* (1970), *Master of Reality* (1971), *Sabbath Bloody Sabbath* (1975) and *Heaven and Hell* (1980), with replacement vocalist Ronnie James Dio, followed in fiendish succession.

Despised by critics and ignored by radio programmers, Sabbath and its special brand of doom and gloom nevertheless sold millions of records. Iommi's radically detuned Gibson SG and his inventive soloing became the major source of inspiration for such guitarists as Edward Van Halen, Kim Thayil and, of course, the young James Hetfield, who went on to co-found the modern-day rock juggernaut, Metallica.

"I discovered Black Sabbath by digging through my older brother's record collection," Hetfield recalls. "Their album covers really drew me in. I immediately thought, 'I gotta put this on.' And when I did, I couldn't believe it. I was like, 'Whoa! Heavy as shit.' Sabbath was everything that the Sixties weren't. Their music was so cool because it was completely anti-hippie. I hated the Beatles, Jethro Tull, Love and all that other happy shit."

Though Black Sabbath has had its ups and downs and endured numerous traumatic personnel changes, Iommi and company are back, stronger than ever, with *Dehumanizer*. The album features a fresh line-up that includes Dio, Butler and veteran drummer Vinny Appice.

"If you like songs like 'War Pigs,' then you'll like this one," Iommi says. "There are a lot of heavy riffs, and it's real raunchy."

That invocation of the very appropriate terms "real" and "raunchy" is a good place to turn to our historic interview with guitar sorcerer Tony Iommi and his second-generation apprentice, James Hetfield. We convened in the booth of a seedy Manhattan bar, where the clientele remained oblivious to the presence, in a secluded rear booth, of two of rock and roll's greatest heavyweights.

GUITAR WORLD: Tony, what were your earliest influences?
TONY IOMMI: In the beginning I was primarily influenced by old blues records. Since liner notes on most blues 78s were either sketchy or non-existent, I never knew who half of the musicians were. I still don't.
GW: What was your first band like?
IOMMI: There were six of us: the four original members of Black Sabbath plus a sax player and a slide guitar player.
JAMES HETFIELD: Was that Earth?
IOMMI: That was before Earth. I think we called ourselves the Pop Top Blues Band, or something equally stupid. We eventually broke up so we could get rid of the sax and slide player. The four of us wanted to move away from the blues thing.
GW: How did you make the jump from playing traditional blues to composing the heavy, riff-oriented music that characterized Sabbath?
IOMMI: Well, to be honest, we just became so fed up with people talking while we were playing that we said, "Screw it, let's turn it up so they won't be able to chatter." [*laughs*] The band just kept getting louder and louder.
GW: Did your new sound provoke an immediate reaction from the audience?
IOMMI: Yeah. After we wrote "Wicked World" and "Black Sabbath," we thought, "Well, we're going to have to try them out." When we did, everybody in the club just froze. We had all these blues people

saying, "What's that?" The reactions were very strong, both pro and con. But I think most people enjoyed what we were doing because they'd never heard anything like it.

HETFIELD: Didn't you guys play "Blue Suede Shoes" for a while?

IOMMI: Oh, you know that? We were getting ready to perform on a British television show, and played "Blue Suede Shoes" during sound check. Ozzy didn't even know the words. He was just goofing around while they worked on the camera angles and whatnot. They said, "Play something," and we just played that. Somehow it got bootlegged. I'm afraid our version is obscenely bad—no one should be subjected to it. [*laughs*]

GW: James, how did Metallica come to pioneer thrash metal?

HETFIELD: Like Tony, we also played cover tunes when we first started. We were really influenced by the New Wave of British Heavy Metal, which included bands like Venom and Diamond Head— underground stuff. We learned a bunch of their songs from a batch of obscure singles that Lars [*Ulrich, drums*] had collected. Most people thought we were performing originals—they had never heard any of the shit before—which was good for us! We took all the credit. You know: "Hey, you guys write good songs," "Yeah, I know." [*laughs*] We certainly weren't going to tell them the truth.

Eventually we started playing everything faster because, just like with Sabbath, the crowd wasn't paying any attention to us and that pissed us off. In L.A., people were just there to drink and see who was there and shit. We decided to try to wake everybody up by playing faster and louder than anybody else.

Nervousness also contributed to our sound. Lars was always nervous on stage, so he'd play faster and faster. That was a huge challenge for us, but nobody wanted to wimp out and tell him that he was playing too fast. We just figured, "Hell, we'll just play fast, too." So it became part of a game.

GW: Did you ever play any Sabbath tunes?

HETFIELD: Not in Metallica, but I did in high school. I'd play Sabbath, Thin Lizzy and some of the heavier stuff at parties.

GW: Tony, in the early days of Sabbath, did you ever feel like you were competing with bands like Deep Purple and Led Zeppelin?

IOMMI: Certainly. There was always competition between Zeppelin, Purple and ourselves. In fact, Robert Plant and John Bonham were from Birmingham, which was our hometown. We all knew each other, which made it worse.

GW: Did you ever jam with Plant or Bonham?

IOMMI: Bonham got up and played with us a few times. In fact, he was my best man when I got married. The main thing I remember about John was that he was in an incredible number of groups. He'd only be in them for a week, and they'd get rid of him because he was too loud. He had this tremendous list of bands that he'd played with written on his bass drum case. Certainly a character!

GW: Was it hard to play in a tough factory town like Birmingham?

IOMMI: It had an effect on us. We were completely surrounded by violence and pollution, so that was a big part of our music. We were living our music.

GW: Weren't you and Ozzy Osbourne actually in different street gangs?

IOMMI: Yeah, I used to hate the sight of Ozzy. I couldn't stand him, and I used to beat him up whenever I saw him. We just didn't get on at school. He was a little punk. It's pretty amazing that he eventually became part of Sabbath. Bill and I were looking for a singer, and we spotted this advert that said, "Singer looking for a gig. Call Ozzy at…" I said to Bill, "I know an Ozzy. It can't possibly be that one." So we went to the address listed in the ad, and knocked on the door. Sure enough, Ozzy appeared.

I said to Bill, "Forget it, forget it." But Bill wanted to chat with him. We talked, and when we left I said, "No way, Bill, I know him." Three weeks later, we ended up together. Life moves in mysterious ways.

GW: What's your craziest Ozzy Osbourne story?

IOMMI: I don't know—there are so many. [*laughs*] Wait, here's one. Actually, it's quite funny. We were all in an elevator in this real plush hotel, and Ozzy decided to take a crap. As he was doing it, the elevator was going down to the reception floor. The door opened suddenly—and there was Ozzy with his pants around his knees. And all these people in fur coats were just staring at him with their mouths open. [*uproarious laughter all around*]

HETFIELD: I heard one story, I don't know if this is true, that Bill Ward showed up to go on tour one time with his only suitcase filled with beer.

IOMMI: Well, Bill never used to take many clothes at all. And when he did, he'd have two suitcases: one with dirty clothes and one with dirtier clothes.

HETFIELD: And tights?

IOMMI: Oh yeah, he always had his red tights.

HETFIELD: What do you think of his tights?

IOMMI: Bill was a character! He was voted the scruffiest, most untidy drummer in England.

GW: Considering the competition, that was quite an achievement!

IOMMI: But it was Bill. He was our outlet, the one everybody picked on. I used to do terrible things to him. I actually set him on fire once—honest to God. We were recording *Heaven and Hell*, and I asked, "Can I set you on fire, Bill?" And he said, "Well, not now, not now." So I said. "Okay," and then forgot all about it.

An hour later Bill said, "Well, I'm going home now. Do you still want to burn me, or what?" I said, "Sure." So I got this bottle of petrol, tipped it on Bill, set fire to him and—*voomph*! I couldn't believe it! He went up like a Christmas tree. Well, he knew I was going to burn him, but he didn't know to what extent. He screamed and started rolling around on the floor. His clothes started burning and his socks melted—the nylon socks stuck to his leg. I wasn't able to help him because I couldn't stop laughing.

It was actually pretty serious; he had to go to the hospital. I felt really bad. He had third-degree burns on his arms and legs and everywhere. The next day his mother phoned me up and said, "You balmy bastard. It's about time you grew up. Our Bill is going to have to have his leg off." She exaggerated a bit. But things like that were a regular occurrence with Bill.

GW: James, many bands have modeled themselves after Metallica.

How does that make you feel?

HETFIELD: It's like being bootlegged. You can't get mad about it, because there is nothing you can do. In a way, it's very complimentary—it's pretty flattering to think that people are taking the time to copy my style. When they get really close to ripping off actual riffs or parts of songs, that's when you have to call them up and say, "Hey, what the hell are you doing?" [*laughs*]

Actually, me and my buddy Bob were talking last night about how bands have gotten really competitive lately. I think it has a lot to do with last summer's Clash of the Titans tour. I didn't like the fact that Megadeth, Anthrax and Slayer were talking shit. Before, the attitude was more like, "Come on, buddy, let's jam." We were fighting for the same cause—getting our music heard. There doesn't seem to be any unity anymore. It's just too damn bad.

IOMMI: It was really much the same in the early Seventies with us and Deep Purple. We were really concerned about who was going to sell more records or chart higher. And you'd say to yourself, "I hope they don't."

HETFIELD: What kind of amps have you used through the years?

IOMMI: I used Laneys for years.

HETFIELD: What did you use for distortion?

IOMMI: Basically, I just used a little box called a Rangemaster, which boosted the input. Now they build that directly into amps, don't they? Believe it or not, I went to several companies 20 years ago and said, "Can you build this into an amp?" They all said, "Don't be stupid, nobody's going to want to buy something that distorts an amplifier." I said, "Of course they will. If they like that sound, they'll buy them. If they don't, they'll buy your ordinary one." And it took them 15 years before they realized what I was saying. In fact, Laney came to me later and said, "Now we know what you were talking about."

HETFIELD: How did you come to use a Gibson SG?

IOMMI: I played a Fender Stratocaster up until the first album. Then, just as we were getting ready to go into the studio, one of the Strat pickups blew. As luck would have it, I had an SG lying around. I'd bought it as a spare, but never played it. At first I was frightened, thinking, "God, I'm going to have to use this one now, and I've never played it." But it worked out fine, and I've used it ever since.

HETFIELD: The same thing happened to me. I was playing a Flying V all the time, and one day the headstock broke. I had an Explorer as a backup guitar, and it just felt right.

GW: Tony, didn't you replace one of the SG's pickups?

IOMMI: Yeah. Over the years I've tried to get various guitar companies involved with me, but none of them really worked out. So I put the money up and bought my own guitar company. I hired a fellow named John Birch to design whatever I needed. John, incidentally, made my first 24-fret guitar. I had approached Gibson, and they said, "We can't make a 24-fret instrument, we're not interested." As soon as they said "can't," I said, "That's it, I'm going to do it." So I got John, who was a bit of an eccentric. He made this guitar, which I've still got at home. Next I said, "This is great! Now we've got to design our own pickup." So we went through a period of trying different pickups. John wound each one differently. And when we found a pickup we really liked, we'd make a few that were very similar. They were never exactly the same, but similar.

GW: James, were you ever interested in custom instruments?

HETFIELD: Never.

IOMMI: The only reason I got involved in guitar-making was because there were few alternatives to the mainstream companies. Now there are lots of guitar companies, pickups, effects and gadgets to choose from. In the Seventies, there was nothing.

HETFIELD: Do you downpick most of your rhythm parts?

IOMMI: Yeah, they sound heavier that way. The big problem with being the only guitarist in the band is that you have to work hard to keep the bottom from falling out. I tried all sorts of things, like creating rhythm parts that would allow the low E string to ring as much as possible. And Geezer played an eight-string bass, which helped for a while.

GW: Although many people credit Edward Van Halen, you were actually one of the first guitarists to detune to an Eb, which helped create your signature dark sound.

IOMMI: People would always tell me, "You can't lower the pitch of your strings, that's not right." I actually used several different tunings. I would try anything. Occasionally, I'd tune as much as three semitones down for Ozzy because he couldn't hit certain notes.

HETFIELD: Wow! So you tuned down to a C sharp or something?

IOMMI: We'd try anything to make our sound heavier.

HETFIELD: Wasn't it hard to stay in tune, especially since you use .008s?

IOMMI: It was. Particularly with my Gibson, because the neck would shift.

HETFIELD: On the other hand, the combination of light strings and detuning must've made it easy for you to bend strings and apply vibrato.

IOMMI: Actually, I had to use light strings. I had a work-related accident in the early Sixties that cut off the tips of my fingers. As a result, I can't bend heavier strings. I can't even feel the strings. [*displays his amputated fingers*] See, this one's cut off, and that one's gone off that way.

HETFIELD: [*visibly shaken*] Wow!

IOMMI: Suddenly, I had to develop a new way of playing. Ironically, I had the accident on the same day that I was supposed to quit my factory job to tour Germany with this group. So when I started playing again, I had to devise a new way. I used to play a lot with my forefinger and pinky because the two middle fingers were bandaged up. I learned to use and bend with my little finger a lot.

HETFIELD: You never tried using your right hand?

IOMMI: Well, I tried, but it was too difficult. I was too impatient to try playing the other way—I just couldn't get the hang of it. As you can imagine, I had to learn to play standard chords in very unorthodox ways. Then I created these plastic thimbles that extended the length of my fingers, which allowed me to play in a normal fashion.

HETFIELD: Why do you need the thimbles? Why can't you just use your shortened fingers?

IOMMI: There's only one layer of skin that covers the bone.

Sometimes when I'm playing with the thimbles they come off and...

HETFIELD: Ouch!

GW: So basically, the accident indirectly led you to develop this completely unique style.

IOMMI: Yeah. I thought I was finished, because I went to different specialists and they all said, "Forget it." Then a friend of mine bought me a record by jazz guitarist Django Rheinhardt and told me to have a listen. I said, "He's really good." Then he told me that Django was able to use only two fingers. It started me to thinking, "Well, he was able to do it. I'm gonna have a go at this." And that's what sort of started me on the way again.

HETFIELD: Did you ever think it would be cool to have another guitar player in the band?

IOMMI: I wouldn't mind it now, but my first experience with the slide player I mentioned earlier was so bad that it left a sour taste in my mouth. He was louder than me, and I felt like we were constantly competing with each other. Actually, Queen's Brian May has played with us.

HETFIELD: Oh, really?

IOMMI: He's the only other guitarist I've really played with. We've done a lot together over the years, and I've really enjoyed it.

GW: James, it must be nice to have another guitar player in the band. Does Kirk offer suggestions when you get stuck for ideas?

HETFIELD: We're a weird pair. We're not as close as two guitar players in a band usually are. We know our limits with each other. He plays the solos. He can play solos and I can't. Actually, I can solo, but I tend to play your standard boxy, blues shit, which I dig. I play all the rhythm tracks and most of the main melodic lines, and Kirk just comes in and does the solos.

GW: Tony, what were your main responsibilities in Sabbath?

IOMMI: I usually wrote the riffs and Geezer wrote the words. We credited everybody because we didn't want to create any competition or ill-will in the band. We wanted everyone to share in the band's success equally. It went on like that for years until Ronnie came in. Unfortunately, my role began to grow. It just became accepted that I was responsible for booking the studios, producing the record, organizing everybody's life. It got pretty out of control.

HETFIELD: So you had a major role in producing Sabbath.

IOMMI: Yeah, but I wasn't really thrilled with the responsibility. The band would come to me and say, "We need a studio. Well, you know about it—which one should we get?" And then they would say, "We don't want any outside people coming in. We'll do it ourselves." And "ourselves" always ended up meaning me. I didn't mind it at first; in fact, I enjoyed it to a point. But it's hard when you start getting too bogged down. All I wanted to do was play and be part of the band. I didn't necessarily want to sit at a mixing board all night. Ultimately, though, it' s probably better to do it yourself than leave it up to a stranger.

GW: James, how does Metallica function?

HETFIELD: We have two people trying to run the band—me and Lars—so we're arguing all the time. The other guys are just like, "Whatever, just put the thing out." Sometimes I think it would be a hell of a lot easier if there was just one of us, but we're a little too stubborn for that.

GW: The latest Metallica record, *Metallica*, sounds great. It's a classic example of a band working well with an outside producer.

HETFIELD: It worked well because the roles were made very clear. We brought Bob Rock in to create a great-sounding record, but we didn't want him messing with our songs. We wanted Bob to take care of the engineering so we could get a little looser with the songs. Still, Lars and I had a real difficult time staying out of his hair. Bob definitely got ruffled quite a few times, but I think he'd work with us again.

GW: Tony, are you meticulous in the studio?

IOMMI: Well, the first album went really quickly.

HETFIELD: Yeah, same with us. Our first album was recorded in no time. We had rehearsed all the songs a million times. And played them live a trillion times.

GW: Is it true that the first Black Sabbath album was recorded in only eight hours?

IOMMI: Yes. On an eight-track machine.

HETFIELD: You beat us!

IOMMI: And the next album, *Paranoid*, was done in only a few days. That was a long time for us; we didn't know anything about studios. Having three or four days to do an album was a complete luxury. But it got worse. The longer we had, the longer it took. The more success you have, the more you start fussing over details, and it takes longer and longer.

HETFIELD: If you don't try everything, it's like, "We could've done that!" It's better to regret doing it than not doing it.

IOMMI: We also became very lazy and self-indulgent. We'd record in Miami or L.A., and everybody'd be down on the beach. "Should we go in today? No, definitely not. We'll go in tomorrow." It got like that. And then you end up taking six months, and you're not really doing anything apart from telling jokes. We fell into that trap a few times.

GW: Tony, when guitarists began using speed-picking and tapping, did you feel any pressure to keep up with the times?

IOMMI: I felt that was good for them, but not for me. I'm not that sort of guitarist—I'm from the old school. I think if I started doing it, it would sound corny.

GW: Why do you think Black Sabbath became a punching bag for the critics? Millions of people loved you.

IOMMI: Millions of people hated us as well. Probably more hated us. A lot of journalists literally hated the sight of us. And it was pretty unusual, really. I think we were the band to pick on from day one because we went against all the things we were supposed to be. Everybody picked on us because we were "Satanic." The Church went against us in a big way.

HETFIELD: Did you ever have to cancel any gigs because of protesters?

IOMMI: Well, the Church stopped a few gigs from happening. One case was quite funny. A church ran a thing in the papers for weeks before a scheduled performance that said, "If you let these lads into town, you're committing a sin." Anyway, they managed to stop us from playing. And the next day that church, for some reason, burned down.

[*laughs*] And guess who got the blame? The uproar was ridiculous!

We get it from the other side, too. One night, after finishing a show, we returned to the hotel and found the corridor leading to our rooms completely filled with people wearing black cloaks, sitting on the floor with candles in their hands, chanting, "Ahh-hh." So we climbed over them to get to our rooms, but could still hear them chanting. We called security, but that didn't work. So we synchronized our watches, opened our doors at the same time, blew the candles out and sang "Happy Birthday" to them. Pissed 'em off. They freaked—they were expecting us to help them conduct a Satanic mass and they got "Happy Birthday" instead.

A worse incident happened in California. When we arrived at the gig, there was a red cross painted on our dressing room door, so we figured, "This must be the room!" [*laughs*] When we were playing, my amp started crackling. I got so pissed that I walked off the stage. As I was walking off, some guy with a dagger lunged at me and tried to stab me. As it turned out, the cross on the door was written in his blood—he had cut up his hands. As they dragged him away he yelled at us, "Satanists!"

GW: Do you ever worry that your music may affect people in a negative way?

IOMMI: There have been bad ones. I think the Son of Sam murders were associated with us because he recited words from our songs when he killed people. So, of course, we got dragged into that court case. In England, a nurse committed suicide, and they found *Paranoid* on her turntable. They took that into court and played it to see if there was any possibility that the music drove her to kill herself.

But, you know, we're used to that. It's been that way since we started. You wouldn't believe some of the letters we've received, and some of the people that have turned up. Admittedly, in the early days of the band we were involved with the head witch in England. He used to come to shows and try to get us to attend his meetings. We checked into some of it out of natural curiosity, but none of us were ever seriously involved with witchcraft or the occult.

GW: James, are you aware of being a role model?

HETFIELD: Yeah. Interviewers always ask for your opinion about this or that, but I'm just an artist doing what I like to do. If anything, we've been telling the kids to think for themselves. People say, "You're a role model for these kids, so you'd better tell them what to do." Hell, no one told me what to do. I hate people telling me what to do!

GW: Both of you have had to deal with personnel changes in your band. Is that kind of change usually positive or negative?

HETFIELD: It depends on the circumstance, of course. Trying to find someone new when [*bassist*] Cliff Burton died was like, "Man, this guy had better be good." We chose Jason [*Newsted*] because he can write, he's really energetic, and he can down-pick as fast as me. [*laughs*] You never know whether you're making the right choice, but getting new blood sure peps you up.

GW: Did Jason get any shit in the beginning?

HETFIELD: He still does. He's been in the band longer than Cliff was, yet he's still the new guy—and it won't change until there's another new guy.

GW: What do you think, Tony? Sabbath has been through many changes.

IOMMI: When Ronnie replaced Ozzy, he definitely injected a lot of positive energy. Ozzy had become predictable. Ronnie had a completely different approach, and I think we worked well as a writing team. I never sat down to write with Ozzy, which is a shame.

GW: James, has it been difficult for Metallica to grow together?

HETFIELD: [*with an intimidating voice*] What are you trying to say? Are you trying to get me to fire people?

GW: [*turning pale*] No, no. Not at all.

HETFIELD: Don't worry, I know what you're getting at. [*laughs*]

IOMMI: My role in the band was to play big brother. If there was a party happening, I wasn't able to go, because I had to set an example. I never wanted that role, but somehow I got it. It's a nasty job, but somebody's got to do it.

HETFIELD: No doubt. We're pretty open as a band, and we tell each other straight up, "That's fucked up." We're pretty sarcastic also. We know each other really well—I mean, shit, we basically grew up together.

IOMMI: We never, ever, had that. We couldn't even exchange riffs. It's only now that Geezer will come to me with riffs and say, "What do you think of this?" "Bloody hell, that's great." And it's good. With our current line-up, we're more at the stage you're at now. We can talk about things, whereas in the past we weren't able to do that. All the years we've been together, we were never able to say, "You're playing crap" or "Do this instead of that." It's gotten much better.

HETFIELD: It's got to be honest and open. You're working for the same team. We ain't playing games here. If something's wrong, speak up. And we do yell at each other. We expect a lot from each other. We all know each other's shit. Kirk plays great lead solos, and he's kind of a quiet guy, so he doesn't raise a big stink. Jason's nuts on stage, he shines there. Lars talks 100 miles an hour during interviews and likes the business part. I yell at people and buy 'em beers. [*laughs*]

Tony, do you ever listen to your old stuff? Do you listen to your albums?

IOMMI: Sure. Occasionally we'll get drunk and think, "What did we used to sound like?" And we'll put an old album on.

HETFIELD: I like listening to our old stuff. The other guys in the band will say things like, "Oh, I can't listen to this song because of such and such note I played." Especially Kirk. I don't do that. I've completely forgotten about things. Either I was drunk or didn't give a shit.

GW: You've remarked in the past that *Ride the Lightning* was your favorite Metallica record. Has *Metallica* surpassed it?

HETFIELD: Yeah, no doubt. I liked *Lightning* because of the muscular sound. The other ones were a little thinner—the songs were good, but the production could've been better.

IOMMI: With every album there are certain bits you like and certain parts you don't like. I think most of our records were good for the time, but you're never satisfied.

HETFIELD: That's the cool thing, though. If you are satisfied, it's over. You gotta keep going. A guitar sound—it's never perfect.

GUITAR WORLD, MARCH 1992

PLEASE HAMMETT, DON'T HURT 'EM

Metallica bruiser Kirk Hammett busts you with the chops that earned him the title, "Best Heavy Metal Guitarist of 1991."

By Nick Bowcott

"**A**LL RIGHT!**"** Kirk Hammett's spontaneous exclamation signals his happiness at the news that *Guitar World* readers had voted him "Best Metal Guitarist" in the magazine's 1991 Readers Poll. "I guess my new approach to playing paid off! I'm very flattered and hope that I can keep on pleasing my fans through Metallica's music."

It has been a good year for Hammett and Metallica. The band's self-titled fifth album has exploded all over the world, entering both the US and UK album charts at Number One, and continues to sell at a pace that would impress even Garth Brooks.

Despite all the mass media attention and superstar status enjoyed by Metallica, Hammett says he and his menacing yet lovable friends still have their hob-nailed boots planted securely on terra firma: "We try not to think about how well the record is selling," he says. "I just concentrate on worrying about day-to-day life—like whether I've had enough sleep for the gig, or whether or not my guitar sound is any good. I tend to live for the moment, and I think it's important to stay that way. I think that when a lot of people reach a certain level of success they get lazy about various things. They start taking their fans for granted, and think that because they're so popular they don't have to play as well because people like their shit anyway! These are dangers that we'll always try our hardest to avoid."

Judging from the way Metallica approach their gigs these days, they run little risk of falling into the "lifestyles of the rich and famous" trap the guitarist is so wary of. The band's performances on their current tour are longer than ever before and, as always, they've been treating their fans like royalty. After thrilling yet another sold-out arena audience with three hours of vintage, pounding Metallica, Hammett, Hetfield, Ulrich and Newsted stayed a good while to sign autographs for a horde of fist-pumping Metalli-heads. Only when everyone was satisfied did an exhausted but exuberant Kirk Hammett come around to celebrate his Readers Poll triumph and share a few moments with *Guitar World*.

GUITAR WORLD: Some exciting new things have been added to your current live show, like the close-ups that appear on the video screens.

KIRK HAMMETT: Instead of your usual rock-star crotch shots, we wanted to capture more interesting things, like my hand positions during a solo or the look in James' eyes when he's singing certain parts.

GW: Speaking of Mr. Hetfield, his vocals sound marvelous—not only on the *Metallica* album, but also on stage. Even the old material benefits greatly from his new-found confidence.

HAMMETT: Absolutely. James has really come a long way with his vocals. It's great to hear him use his voice in so many different ways. I love the way he sings on the album, and you're right about our older material—a lot of it sounds way better now. He even warms up his voice before we go on, which is something he never used to do. Basically, he's become much more serious about that part of his gig, and it's paying dividends.

What did you think of our new stage set-up?

GW: It's excellent. Although you don't have any back line, the stage never looked empty because you made full use of the available space. But I imagine it must take a lot out of you physically—especially with a set that lasts nearly three hours!

HAMMETT: Yeah, it's a pretty intense workout. To prepare for a show, we each warm up our hands, then we all get together in the dressing room and stretch for about 15 minutes. That actually is beneficial to my guitar playing, because playing on a stage like this is a physical activity. Your hands could be as warmed up as possible, but if you aren't warmed up, you're going to feel it, and it could affect your guitar work as well as your overall performance

GW: The "snake pit" [*a sunken area in the middle of Metallica's stage, where 100 people are able to view the show from the band's perspective*] is a great idea. Who is selected to have those tickets?

HAMMETT: Most of them are local radio contest winners. We also have a guy who goes up to the nosebleed section and asks kids if they want to trade their ticket for a place in the pit. Interestingly, people often say, "No, I don't wanna move!"

GW: I was also impressed that all of you spent two hours after the performance with your fans. The band obviously holds its audience in extremely high regard.

HAMMETT: We like to keep in touch with our fans. It's important to come into direct contact with them, so we can get a vibe as to how the show feels from off the stage. We respect their opinions greatly—and we don't always hear favorable things. But that's good, because you have to take both viewpoints equally seriously. You can't always pretend that everything's perfect.

GW: Thanks to the camera close-ups we discussed earlier, I know you use your left-hand pinky a great deal.

HAMMETT: When I first learned to play, someone told me, "Hey, you better use your little finger, or it's just gonna hang out there." I've used it ever since. It definitely helps me play certain wide-stretch things that I probably couldn't reach if I were just a three-fingered player.

GW: You have a very precise, speedy right-hand picking technique. How did you develop it?

HAMMETT: Well, one thing that I've noticed over the years is that there are basically two distinct approaches to picking. There are those who pick with their wrist, and then there are those who pick with their whole forearm. I've found that you have a lot more control over your picking when you pivot from your wrist, as opposed to pivoting from your elbow, because there's just a lot less overall movement going on. By picking this way you can fine-tune your right-hand technique into a very precise and controlled wrist maneuver.

Getting this picking approach down can really make a big difference—especially to your rhythm playing in very fast songs. As you probably know, most of our rhythm work is done using downpicking only, even some of the very fast stuff. That's another reason why it's good to come from the wrist. Also, when you pick by moving your forearm it's a lot harder to palm-mute the strings by the bridge. But when you pivot from your wrist it's easy to get that palm-muted "chunk" happening with your right hand because it's hardly moving.

GW: I imagine that one of the advantages of using a lot of downstrokes is that artificial, pick-induced harmonics are easier to produce.

HAMMETT: Absolutely. I also find that using mostly downstrokes gives me more attack and subtlety. For instance, when you're playing a bunch of passing notes, you can make them softer until you want one to really jump out, even when it isn't an artificial harmonic.

GW: I've noticed that although you occasionally do a lot of hammering-on and pulling-off when playing fast, you frequently pick almost every note of your high-speed solos.

HAMMETT: Yeah, as far as playing fast is concerned, I've noticed a lot of my friends only pick every third or fourth note; they slur [*hammer-on, pull-off, bend, slide or tap*] the rest. So I've gotten into that habit over the past few years. I used to pick virtually every note in my leads and just slur every once in a while because I found that I have a lot more attack that way and I can get more accents and convey percussive ideas. Though I do like the legato feel you can achieve with hammer-ons and pull-offs, I think that you have to be able to pick fast runs to be a well-rounded player.

Whenever I'm doing a bend, a pull-off or a hammer-on, I always go into it with a downstroke. In fact, a lot of my soloing revolves purely around downpicking.

GW: Compared to the shredding of your past, a good deal of your playing on the new album is pretty laid back and "slow handed." What brought about this dramatic change of direction?

HAMMETT: Basically I just decided to say, "Screw everyone around me—from now on I'm just gonna play what I think is important to me and our music." So I gave the big finger to all the current trends in technical wizardry and just went off and did what I felt was best for the songs.

GW: Would you say this indicates that you've matured as a musician?

HAMMETT: Yeah, definitely. I still enjoy playing in that high-tech way, but I just felt that there was a big need for a change. I didn't want to fall into the trap of competing with all these other great guitar players. I just wanted to side-step that whole thing and get out of the race! [*laughs*]

Also, the band as a unit has changed a great deal—we're a lot more cohesive and there's a lot more space in our new material. Consequently, I thought, "Why stop there? Why don't I also change my style, which will help the overall picture look that much more different?"

GW: If the *Metallica* album is any indicator, the whole band is obviously very comfortable with this new approach.

HAMMETT: Absolutely. We were very comfortable with *Ride the Lightning, Master of Puppets* and *Kill 'Em All.* But we were slightly uncomfortable with *...And Justice for All.* I think we were chasing our tails a bit back then. Now we're well and truly back on the right track.

GW: Has this new outlook of yours affected the way you practice the instrument?

HAMMETT: Yes it has. I no longer look at the guitar neck as a bunch of patterns and scales. As a result, I find myself playing more off-the-cuff. When we started preparing for this tour, we began rehearsing songs that I hadn't played for a while, and I'd completely forgotten the guitar solos! But instead of going back and relearning them, I decided to just play something different every night, which makes it a lot more exciting for me because I'm not stuck in any ruts—I can't walk out on stage and play the same "safe" guitar solo at every show. I'd rather be able to play however I feel. Obviously, some nights it might not be as good as others, but when I really pull it off and actually express what I want, it's much more rewarding.

GW: So you're not one of those guys who thinks it's important to duplicate recorded solos because that's what the audience expects to hear?

HAMMETT: Well, despite what I've just said, I actually do think that way! There are certain things people simply want to hear. With the new material, I pretty much stick to what's on the album. Over the course of the tour, things will evolve and I'll change a note here and a phrase there. It's mostly on the older material that I'm just playing off-the-cuff. There are a few things in the new stuff where, when we play live, I can't remember how I played in the studio—the second solo in "Wherever I May Roam," for example. But I know the key bits, and then I improvise around them.

This approach has made a huge difference for me, because no two gigs are the same. The same applies to my open guitar solo; I haven't really stuck to any format apart from the two ensemble pieces I play—"Funeral Dance for a Marionette," the Metallica arrangement of the Alfred Hitchcock movie theme, and "Mistreated."

GW: I really enjoyed hearing your version of that. I love Deep Purple's original, too.

HAMMETT: Ssshhh! No one knows what it is! [*laughs*] It's amazing, I guess a lot of kids who hear me play it think it's something of mine. I wish! The live version Blackmore does on Deep Purple's *Made in Europe* album is particularly incredible.

Anyhow, getting from A to B in the open solo is different for me every night. The frustrating thing is that I always sit down in the dressing room before the gig and say, "Okay, I'm gonna play this lick and this lick and this lick." But it never works out like that. It's different every single night, and it bugs me! [*laughs*] I know that eventually it'll take shape, just like it has on past tours.

GW: Though you maintain that you've opted to retire from the "technical-guitar-playing race," I'd say that, from watching you play tonight, it's clear that you still enjoy blazing out the odd lightning fast lick.

HAMMETT: Absolutely. The difference is that I tend to use speed as a texture nowadays. Knowing when to play fast and when to play slow, and being able to mix it up, makes all the difference in the world. There are certain guitar players who are basically one-speeded, and their playing sounds flat and one-dimensional. It's good to strive to be three-dimensional, so that what you play has a lot of ups and downs, dips and so forth.

GW: Who, in your opinion, are masters of this sort of three-dimensional playing?

HAMMETT: Jimi Hendrix, Jimmy Page and Joe Satriani. Joe is the master—when I first met him, that's the one thing that just completely took me aback. I remember thinking to myself, "God, this guy is the best guitar player I've ever seen." I knew that one day he was going to be at the top, and when he finally got there I was incredibly happy for him.

GW: What would your advice be to a young soloist with regard to attaining "chops" but not relying on them too heavily?

HAMMETT: Learn as much as you can, but when it comes down to the moment throw it all out the window and play from inside yourself. I think that playing what you feel at the moment is really important. It doesn't matter if you know a billion scales or just two; trying to capture that emotion and putting it across is the name of the game. As far as I'm concerned, if you manage to channel your feelings through your playing, and whoever is listening understands the message, you've succeeded as a musician.

To achieve this goal you've basically got to be yourself and try to be more fluid with your feelings. You shouldn't always use scales as the middle man between your heart and your hands, because sometimes all that knowledge can be a barrier to what you really want to say. If you can eliminate that middle man, and just have a constant thought process that flows from your head, through your fingers and out your amp, that's the whole battle won right there.

GW: With all you've achieved in terms of chart success, critical acclaim and public recognition, are their any goals left for you to conquer as a guitarist?

HAMMETT: Hell yeah! As I was telling a friend of mine yesterday, I'm still trying to figure it all out! [*laughs*] After all these years, the instrument is still a mystery to me. I listen to all these great players and think, "God, they're tapping into something I still haven't found." And that's my ambition right there—to find that elusive source.

GUITAR WORLD, APRIL 1993

CLASS REUNION

Joe Satriani and his onetime pupil Kirk Hammett reunite for a little bit of reminiscence, a little bit of Hendrix worship and a little bit of Ice-T.

By Steffan Chirazi

THEY ARE TWO of rock's most celebrated guitarists, but once they were teacher and student. Today, Joe Satriani and his former star pupil Kirk Hammett are old friends. Upon meeting at Hammett's spacious Berkeley, California, home, the two men exchange greetings and quickly catch up on each other's lives—the biggest news being the recent arrival of Satch's first child, Zachariah. But it doesn't take long before the focus of their conversation turns to their mutual obsessions: the guitar and, more specifically, Jimi Hendrix.

"I was only six years old when I first became aware of Hendrix," Hammett recalls. "I was probably more interested in his album covers than his music. I remember thinking that the jacket art of *Are You Experienced?* was amazing. As a kid you tend to overlook big things for silly little things."

"I just remember hearing Hendrix's music coming from one of those big Magnavox music systems, and the whole room started doing tunnel vision," says Satriani. "I walked towards the speaker, my mouth open, and my sister asked, 'What's wrong with you?' I was totally hooked! Jimi's music completely warped my brain, and from then on I was completely pyschedelicized. It was like something happened inside of me, and I never heard anything the same after that."

"He was like [*jazz saxophonist*] John Coltrane—one of music's true innovators," adds Hammett. "He invented a whole new way of composing and recording."

"Plus he was a snappy dresser!" injects Satriani. Hammett grins.

They adjourn to an upstairs room where, amid a porta-studio/computer setup, a conversation begins in earnest. Out of deference to his former guru, Hammett enthusiastically volunteers to conduct the interview. Satriani immediately picks up a guitar, which he proceeds to strum, pick and pluck throughout the entire chat.

KIRK HAMMETT: Joe, tell us about your early days—before the release of your first solo album, *Not of This Earth* (Relativity).

JOE SATRIANI: I was playing around San Francisco with a band called The Squares. We were real serious about what we were zoning in on. We thought we were really unique.

HAMMETT: How much of your early material from The Squares made it onto your solo albums?

SATRIANI: None of it. "Can't Slow Down" [*Flying in a Blue Dream*] would've been a really good poppy, psychedelic, Squares-type song. We liked bands like the Gang of Four and The Police—we were influenced by anybody who did great pop. We were really prolific. If we played a song at a club on Friday and it went down badly, it was outta there, and we'd start something new in rehearsal the next day.

HAMMETT: Metallica works in the opposite way. We usually start by going through tapes of riffs and rough ideas. Then we take the cream of the crop and develop them until we end up with something we like. We never throw out songs. We just hammer away until we have a finished product. What it does is leave a lot of leftover riffs—but not songs.

Joe, what are your feelings about the current guitar scene?

SATRIANI: There's a lot happening right now. Anti-technique is back.

HAMMETT: When you say "anti-technique," are you referring to bands like Nirvana?

SATRIANI: It could be anyone in the Top Five, from Billy Ray Cyrus to Nirvana. No matter who it is, they are part of a never-ending cycle of action and reaction. But my feeling is that you shouldn't follow trends just to follow them. It's better to be 100 percent committed and dead wrong. More than likely, one day you'll find yourself on the right side if you stick with what you do.

HAMMETT: I agree with that. It's better to stick to what you believe in. But getting back to the question of technique vs. anti-technique, I think one of the reasons there's this continual cycle of styles is because musicians get tired of hearing things more quickly than the public. It seems musicians are always doomed to rebel against popular trends. Guitar players in the Nineties seem to be reacting against the technique-oriented Eighties.

SATRIANI: But it's too bad that guitarists feel they have to reject the whole school of technical playing. There are guitarists who reach their artistic heights through technique. Other people are just better at writing three-minute songs.

GUITAR WORLD: Jamming seems to be a lost art.

HAMMETT: We toured with the Black Crowes briefly in 1990, and they were the only band I'd ever seen play a blues in E for 15 minutes. I have the utmost respect for them. They played in front of a Russian audience that didn't even know how to react to any of us, and I was amazed that people really liked it.

Obviously, if you go to a blues or jazz gig the fans are more accustomed to long instrumentals.

SATRIANI: God, yeah. Blues fans wanna see you do it. When you play a blues gig, you really have to spill some blood!

HAMMETT: I remember seeing you play a phenomenal improvised solo in concert using controlled feedback. I always wanted to compliment you on that. It's so hard to find the right spot at the right volume where a note will feed back in the right way.

SATRIANI: Are you familiar with Hendrix's 1967 performance at the Monterey Pop Festival? He did the most beautiful feedback solo I've ever heard in my life! He plays a symphony there; it's just unbelievable.

A funny story from when I played with Mick Jagger on his solo Japanese tour: "Foxy Lady" was part of the set. The hardest part of playing that song is getting the opening bit of feedback to sustain properly. The only way I could do it was by kneeling down in front of a cabinet while leaning back on my toes in this really uncomfortable manner. Then I would have to wait for Mick to take it from that point. This one night I was stuck in this uncomfortable position for over a minute, looking at Mick. I was about to get desperate because I was starting to cramp, when suddenly I just fell back right into the speaker, which created a sudden WEEEEEEE-BOOOMPH! It was pretty funny. Of course, Mick had no idea what was going on; he probably thought I was just improvising or something.

GW: Joe, I've heard you say that when you were teaching, you were able to see where the next generation of players was heading.

SATRIANI: Oh yeah, it was very cool because you saw things starting way before the public ever heard them. When Steve Vai was taking lessons from me, he was already beginning to work on an "Eruption"-style thing. Suddenly, I discovered lots of students messing around with tapping. Then Eddie Van Halen came along and put it all into context—adding some real dynamics and a few other elements. It was the same with you, Kirk—I heard the evolution of thrash before anyone knew what it was.

HAMMETT: Remember when I introduced you to that Yngwie Malmsteen demo? I was like, "Hey Joe, check this out!" "Dark Star" was part of the demo, and we just sat there and listened to it over and over. And in two years everybody was doing it.

SATRIANI: Yeah, that style was assimilated so quickly, and then it just suddenly peaked.

GW: So both of you basically agree that Malmsteen did have his unique and supremely talented day.

HAMMETT: He was great, but it wasn't entirely new, because people like Ulrich Roth were doing it before him.

GW: Kirk, what were you looking for when you took lessons from Joe?

HAMMETT: How to achieve certain sounds. I used to bring him guitar solos and we'd go through them and tear them apart.

SATRIANI: Kirk had a tremendous appetite for all sorts of scales, and his ear knew the differences between them.

HAMMETT: We also used to discuss everyday life. When I first saw you play, I remember thinking it was a crime that you weren't making records and touring. When I saw your rise—which was pretty quick—I was very, very happy.

SATRIANI: From my point of view, my rise was actually pretty slow. I recorded *Not of This Earth* between '84 and '85, using a credit card, and it didn't come out until '87. That was two years of waiting right there. I was on the edge for a long time. I had maxed out my credit card, and had no real money coming in until I joined Greg Kihn's band. [*San Francisco musician Greg Kihn had several hits in the early Eighties, most notably "Jeopardy."—GW ed.*] I got the call from Greg the same week the credit card company started threatening heavily. I went in, played, got some bail-out money. It was funny, because whenever I played *Not of This Earth* for the band, they were thoroughly unimpressed.

Right around that time I also got an audition to join a hard rock band called Giuffria. But then I realized they were this "hair" band, and I wasn't into that at all. I wanted to make that immediately clear. I had very short hair then, and when I went down there to play they were kind of cynical, too. I must've looked incredibly "Bay area" to these L.A. guys.

So, to me, it never really seemed like a meteoric rise. When *Surfing* finally became popular in 1988, I felt a mixture of achievement and relief.

HAMMETT: Joe, would you say your music is spiritually driven?

SATRIANI: I'm always trying to reach people with a message; it's important for me to spread something positive. I have a responsibility to get all those emotions out and across to people, from my spirit to somebody else's. For example, I could never write a song like "Cop Killer" by Body Count. That goes against everything I stand for in terms of being a performer. I couldn't go out in front of thousands of people and encourage violence.

I've been a performer for a long time. You have this power open to you: If you want people to clap their hands, they will; if you want people to shout, they will. I know I can create a domino effect of good will, and help people get through a negative experience by confronting darker emotions.

But to go out and endorse violence in the same way you'd say "everybody put your hands together" is going beyond the limit. Why risk even one person getting killed? Is creating controversy to further your career that important? I mean, let's be honest—Kirk sells records, I sell records and so does Ice-T. But I wouldn't use that platform to spread a message like "kill the police." I mean, he can take out an ad in *The New York Times*, he can speak on public access cable TV, he can do whatever he wants. But if he gets in front of a crowd and talks about killing people...

GW: Do you feel any obligation to say things on stage like, "Get out and vote?"

SATRIANI: No, I don't bother with that. I just live my life as an American citizen and do my bit in my own way. When people have spent hard-earned money to come and see me play, they don't want to hear a preacher. And I don't want to be one. I come to play! I want to spread good vibes with my music; that's what Joe Satriani is all about. And to answer Kirk's question, that is how I express my spirituality. That's all I'm concerned with—making my music a deep and rich experience.

GW: Kirk, do you feel the same responsibility that Joe does?

HAMMETT: Well, I think Ice-T takes it for granted that "Cop Killer" is just a song—that it's merely entertainment. I've never talked to him about it, but he's actually very mellow and very personable— which surprised the hell out of me.

SATRIANI: Which makes it all the more frightening!

GW: Is there a difference between Robert DeNiro playing a psycho in a film and Ice-T portraying one on stage?

SATRIANI: There's a big difference between being an actor and being a musician. Musicians have more responsibility because they're seen as being there just to play music, whereas it is taken for granted that an actor is a character. And do you know what? The Body Count record sucks! When that whole controversy broke, nobody reviewed the actual record. I mean it's admirable that he's trying to fuse rap and thrash, but hey, knock-knock, hello—the record sucks! Shouldn't that be the end of it? Nobody commented on the music, the songs, the performances.

Let me tell you a story. I was told about this guy, a *Flying in a Blue Dream* fanatic, who came from a troubled home. His two favorite songs were "Flying in a Blue Dream" and "I Believe." Whenever he met someone, he'd play them those songs and talk about what the music meant. These two songs were his salvation. So I guess this guy went home to finally try and confront his family problems and all that kind of stuff, and he wound up dying in a mysterious car accident. They ended up putting a tape of it in the coffin, and his whole family remembers him through "I Believe." Can you imagine what it felt like for me—sitting at home, working on guitar, looking after the baby—to hear about that?

HAMMETT: We've had situations like that too. This guy's theme song was "Nothing Else Matters." He ended up dying in a car crash while he was drunk. The lyrics to "Nothing Else Matters" were put on his tombstone, which is pretty heavy.

SATRIANI: The point is that people take your music and end up using it in the most profound way. And you can never think of abusing that privilege of communication between people.

GW: Where does guitar go from here?

HAMMETT: I think technology's going to be even more prevalent in guitar. Industrial music is getting more and more popular, as bands like Ministry and Nine Inch Nails and Godflesh are bringing computers to the forefront.

SATRIANI: I agree with Kirk. But whatever style comes in vogue, there are always gonna be people who stand up and say, "That isn't soulful enough," and retain a traditional sense. Things always go in circles.

HAMMETT: I think the world is ready for another Hendrix.

Michael Uhll/Ebet Roberts

GUITAR WORLD, JULY 1996

BORN AGAIN

Five years have passed since Metallica released the epic "Black Album." During that time, the music world has radically changed—and so has Metallica.

By Tom Beaujour

"**W**HEN WE WERE making our last record, nobody even knew who the fuck Kurt Cobain was!" Kirk Hammett, at ease in the lounge of the New York City recording studio where he and the rest of Metallica are rushing to finish their sixth album, *Load*, is acutely aware of how much the musical climate has changed in the five years since the band put out their last studio recording.

In the late summer of 1991, when *Metallica* was released, "smelling like teen spirit" was still something to be avoided at all costs. A few short months later, Nirvana's *Nevermind* had turned the music world on its head.

With its metallic sheen and top-dollar production values, *Metallica* (known as the "Black Album" to the initiated) stuck out like a sore thumb in grunge's raw sonic landscape. Yet, powered by timeless metal anthems like "Enter Sandman" and "The Unforgiven," it sold in excess of eight million copies, in the process turning Metallica into one of the biggest—if not *the* biggest—bands in the world. As it turned out, it was also heavy metal's swan song, or at least the last recording to be successfully marketed as "metal." Today, *Metallica* stands as the last towering monument to an era marked by bombast and excess.

When it came time to make *Load*, Metallica clearly felt the need to find a new, more forward-thinking sound. "A lot of bands get stuck staring at their own belly buttons," says vocalist/guitarist James Hetfield. "They're like, 'Wow, we made such a good record last time. We've got to keep doing this.' We won't do that. The whole point of Metallica is to come up with fresh shit."

Perhaps nothing reflects Metallica's embrace of Nineties musical values more than the band's striking new hairstyles, although both guitarists are reluctant to attribute significance to the cosmetic change: "I had fucking long hair for 20 years! Of course I cut it!" grumbles Hammett.

Metallica's new 'dos, however, are peanuts compared to the musical makeover undergone by the band. *Load* is a fiercely modern album, combining the moody melodicism of Seattle's best bands with the skull-splitting crunch that only Metallica can deliver. It's also the first album on which Hammett shares rhythm guitar duties with Hetfield.

"We wanted to get a looser sound on this record, and the best place to do that was with the guitars," Hetfield explains. "It was a little nerve-wracking at first. I felt like there was too much new shit happening in Metallica at once. And that was probably the newest thing of all, besides our stupid haircuts."

Hammett also approached the new guitar regime with a degree of trepidation. "I was actually feeling very self-conscious about it, because I didn't want to step on James' turf," he says. "But it turned out a lot better than I thought it would, and it adds a great texture to the mix." The new division of labor, which yields slyly intertwining parts, is more closely related to the telepathic guitar interplay of the Rolling Stones than to the battering-ram riffery of Judas Priest or Diamond Head.

While amply packed with heavy fare, *Load* also finds Metallica exploring new sounds and previously unexplored genres. Songs like "2x4," with its Aerosmith-like swagger, and "Ain't My Bitch," which rocks to a ZZ Top-on-steroids groove, reflect the band's new-found ability to incorporate Hetfield's love of Southern rock and Hammett's blues jones into Metallica's patented grind. Hypnotic, pop-tinged offerings like "Hero of the Day" and "Mama Said," a startlingly lush, swirling anthem, also indicate that Hetfield has vastly expanded the emotional range of his vocal delivery. In so doing, he firmly establishes himself as one of the premier rock voices of the Nineties, along with a handful of others like Kurt Cobain, Alice in Chains' Layne Staley and Soundgarden's Chris Cornell.

And bands like Soundgarden, of which Hammett and Hetfield are both staunch admirers, are the company that Metallica intends to keep. This summer, Metallica will headline the Lollapalooza tour, sharing the bill with Cornell and company, the Ramones, Rancid and a host of other alternative rock bands. "I think that the bill on this year's Lollapalooza is pretty good," says Hammett. "It may be a little top-heavy because of us and Soundgarden, but it's certainly stronger than last year's. Fuck all those fucking elitists who say 'Metallica's not alternative' or 'They're too big of a band to play Lollapalooza.' They're just being narrow-minded."

Hetfield's take on why Metallica belongs on Lollapalooza is a bit more succinct:

"Uh, next guitar question, please."

GUITAR WORLD: How long have you been working on *Load*?
JAMES HETFIELD: It's been a long time, man. We started in April or May of last year. We worked on writing the songs for three or four months and just kept going and going. We had tons of material, stuff we had accumulated from five years of not writing. First it was like, "Okay, let's stop at 20 songs." Then we'd get going and say, "All right, we'll stop at 30."

It was fuckin' crazy, man. All this material had built up on the road. There were bags and bags of tapes with riffs on them. Sifting through all that shit was difficult.

GW: Did you record more songs than those that are slated to appear on *Load*?
HETFIELD: We recorded quite a few drum tracks, I think 28 in all. We were thinking of doing a double record, but as time went on we

realized that we couldn't tackle all of it at once; we were like nine months into the recording and weren't even done with half of the songs. It was too hard to focus, too much to swallow.

GW: Do you think that you'll use some of the drum tracks on your next album?

HETFIELD: Oh, definitely. That'll be the next record. The tour for this album is supposed to last one year—no more. When we're done with that we'll go into the studio to finish up the 15 or 16 songs that we've already started. Hopefully, they'll still sound good to us then. If we like them, we like them; if not, we'll revamp them, add to them or do whatever it takes. But our feeling right now is that there are some good songs waiting to be finished.

GW: It sounds like you're eager to accelerate your touring and recording cycle.

HETFIELD: Five years between records is too crazy. We don't want to do that anymore. It's getting to be too fucking ridiculous—people waiting for new material forever, us touring too long, killing ourselves. We have to shorten these things up.

Unfortunately, it's really difficult to shorten the tours. People don't realize how global the music market has become. There didn't used to be a fucking Indonesia to play; there wasn't a South Africa, an India or a fucking Turkey. Now there is, and we want to be there. [*laughs*] We're going to have to miss a lot of places we hit on the last tour in order to be back in a year.

GW: The listening public's tastes have shifted radically since you made your last album.

HETFIELD: They've completely shifted since we started writing the songs for *this* record!

KIRK HAMMETT: In the time between albums, we watched all this shit fly by and wondered, "How does Metallica fit into this?" And then we realized that we didn't fit into it at all, never have, and never really will.

GW: Were you influenced by any of the grunge or alternative music that followed Nirvana's *Nevermind* down the pipeline?

HAMMETT: The only real influence that the music I've been hearing has had is that it's sparked my interest in all the old, shitty-sound-ing Electro-Harmonix and MXR effects pedals I used to use when I was younger. But I listened to a lot of that Seattle stuff before it became mega-popular. When it got that big, I stopped.

HETFIELD: [*to Hammett*] Why? Did they suddenly become shitty when they got popular?

HAMMETT: No. I just felt that I couldn't get away from it.

HETFIELD: That happened to me. When the "Black Album" got pop-ular, I stopped listening to it. [*laughs*]

GW: That album has sold eight million copies to date and is still on the charts. What—if any—are the drawbacks of having such a huge hit on your hands?

HETFIELD: Everything gets so inflated. Everything is "More! More! More!" More touring, more interviews—more of everything. Everyone wants something—always. They can't just take you for who you are.

Luckily for us, success wasn't a night and day thing. We had taken a few steps on our way up, so we were able to handle it men-tally. No one in Metallica ended up shooting himself or shooting up, or whatever it is people sometimes feel the need to do in these sit-uations. You see it every fuckin' day in this weird-ass business.

I mean, everyone has their little things that they need to do to release pressure. When you're touring for that long, there's shit that just happens to your head. Sometimes you stray, and hopefully you've got a band that will help you through. We're really lucky to have stuck around this long without having any major crises. I mean, we've had people die in the band and things like that [*origi-nal bassist Cliff Burton was killed in a tour bus accident in 1986*], but as far as people pulling and tugging and fucking with shit, there haven't been too many problems.

It amazes me how certain bands fall apart. It's like, "Fuck, man! Can't you see that shit coming?" But sometimes they don't. It's hard to keep a band uniform and still maintain a comfortable degree of individuality; you have to respect each other all the time.

GW: When you do get some time off, what do you do? Do you get as far away from music as possible?

HETFIELD: I go in cycles. I won't bother listening to music for quite a while, and then I'll feel down or shitty or something and realize that it's because I haven't picked up my guitar or played music. I've conditioned myself to need this stuff for so long that I can't be away from it for too long. It's like, "Whoa, I've got to pick up the guitar and start playing." And it's scary when you haven't played for quite a while and can't remember the riff to "Seek and Destroy!"

I've noticed that it's hard to figure out what you want to do when you come off a two-year tour. While you're out on the road, you make up this list of things that you want to do when the tour's over, and then when you get home you end up vegging. It's a strange feeling to be out on your own again, not to have the Metallica family around you. There's no tour manager to wake me up and tell me to do this or that. It's like, "Whoa! I have to start doing shit for myself here and deciding what I want to do." And then when I finally get it together and start doing all the shit I planned to, it's time to get back to Metallica again.

Sometimes you get torn between the two worlds. Especially when you get to our age, you start to develop a family life and get things kinda going. No one in the band is married or has kids or anything, but you have a girlfriend and your little sanctuary at home, and you've got to keep that together.

But Metallica is the fucking world to me—it always has been, and that's not going to change. Whoever becomes my partner through life has got to deal with that. I'm married to Metallica.

GW: The last two Metallica albums had specific musical agendas. ...*And Justice for All* (1988) was an exercise in taking the complex, challenging arrangements of *Ride the Lightning* (1984) and *Master of Puppets* (1986) to their most elaborate extreme, while *Metallica* was an exercise in economy...

HETFIELD: Economy, my ass! [*laughs*] That was the most expensive record we've ever made.

GW: ...in which you reigned in your song structures and focused on crafting more concise rock songs. What were your goals for this album?

HETFIELD: We wanted to attain a certain degree of looseness with this record. The drums are pretty much as anal as ever, but the vocals, and particularly the guitars, breathe a lot more. Instead of me playing all of the rhythm guitars and trying to double them as closely as possible, like I'd done on our previous albums, both Kirk and I play contrasting rhythm parts on almost all of the record. There isn't really much of that one-dimensional wall of heavy guitar—with a clean guitar coming in once in a while—that we've had on previous albums. I wanted a "medium" sound, if there is such a thing. I was like, "How do I get that? I fucking don't know."

GW: Was it decided before you began recording that both of you would play rhythm guitar on this album?

HAMMETT: No. It was never really something that we spoke about. The first mention of it came while we were recording the drum tracks. When we do that, we all play the songs together in a single room, but the only thing that goes onto the multitrack is the drums—everything else just gets taped. Some of the songs were sounding so good on those tapes that James was like, "Well, maybe Kirk should play on the final version of some of these."

Later on, on a day when James happened to be away on a hunting trip, I was laying down a couple of solos, and when I finished the lead on one of the tunes our producer, Bob Rock, said, "Okay, tune up and we'll do the rhythm for this song now." I was like, "What?"

HETFIELD: By the time I came back, Kirk had put down rhythm tracks on four songs.

HAMMETT: I specifically went out of my way to come up with a second guitar part that would complement James', not ape it. Not that the riffs weren't interesting. The riffs are the riffs—they're the most important part of the song.

Our parts have a really good sense of interplay. And you can actually separate the two guitars and tell who's playing what. James is on the left side, and I'm on the right.

GW: James, was it difficult for you to surrender control?

HAMMETT: I don't think it's a control issue as much as it used to be.

It's more that we're all here to accomplish a common goal.

HETFIELD: It was what was needed for the record. The looseness just wasn't coming across. No matter how many fucking martinis I had, I could never get the guitar tracks to sound different enough. It was the same guitar player playing it fucked up. It wasn't a fucked-up guitar player trying to play it right. [*laughs*]

Basically, no matter how close Kirk plays the riff to the way I did, it won't sound the same, because it's his fingers, his style and his attitude. I would lay a basic scratch track of what I thought the other guitar should be, and Kirk would come in, listen to the track and then do his own thing with it, which was cool.

GW: In the past, was the fact that Kirk didn't get to play rhythm guitar on the records a source of tension within the band?

HAMMETT: Not really. In fact, on this album we argued more about the solos than anything else. But we're always arguing about something, so it was just par for the course.

HETFIELD: I often have a pretty specific idea of what the solo to a particular song should sound like, so it throws me for a loop when Kirk comes in with something else. But then everyone sits down, we talk it out and work out a middle ground that everyone can be happy with. You don't want to have something on a record that someone in the band is going to go insane over and hate.

HAMMETT: We try and resolve things right away, so that two years from now no one will say something sarcastic to the other person about it.

HETFIELD: Well, they probably will anyway. But at least there won't be too much fuel behind it.

GW: What were the bones of contention?

HETFIELD: "Is that in key? Are you sure that's in key?" [*laughs*]

HAMMETT: I had to sit down and explain my approach. I probably have the most open mind of anyone in Metallica, as far as music is concerned. I like a lot of different stuff, and so, occasionally, I'll take an idea inspired by something sort of "out" and bring it to the band. I won't bring it to the band unless I think that there's a chance that they'll like it, and 90 percent of the time they do. But there's that

10 percent of the time where they question it.

On this album, there was one song—which will remain nameless to protect the innocent—where the solo that I played had such a different type of feel that it changed that entire piece of the song. We spent hours debating it, and I literally had to walk James through every single note. There was something about it that he just didn't like, which he thought might have been a harmonic thing. But then we realized that it was just the general sound of the solo. Then James came up with something—like five notes—that colored what I had played sufficiently to make it work for him too.

GW: Your solos on this album are very textured.

HAMMETT: I would hate to say that I'm bored with the standard rock guitar solo, but I've done it for five albums now, and this time I wanted to go in a completely different direction. I wasn't interested in showing off anymore. I wanted to play something that fit the song more like a part than a solo per se, something that had the power to establish a completely different mood in the section of the song that was allocated to me.

When I play at home, I have a Lexicon Jam Man sampling delay with which I can create loops on which to layer guitar textures. That's why things like the Roland VG-8 and the guitar synth are so interesting to me—they put so many sounds at my disposal.

Don't get me wrong, though, I still listen to Jimi Hendrix, Stevie Ray Vaughan, Buddy Guy, Robert Fripp and Adrian Belew. I'm still way into that type of guitar playing. I just don't feel the need to play that way within the context of Metallica anymore.

GW: You've also almost abandoned your wah pedal, which you used on most of the solos on the last album.

HAMMETT: I didn't notice that until just the other day. I was laying down a wah track, and I said to Bob, "Guess what? We don't have the problem we had on the last album. You don't have to hide the wah pedal anymore."

GW: The slide solo on "Ain't My Bitch" is a first for you.

HAMMETT: We wanted to find something different for that song, not just another guitar solo. The slide was really effective because it's such a new sound for us. It's only recently that I've felt comfortable enough with my slide work to actually commit to playing it on the record. I've been working on it for years now—it's not an easy thing to do. I'm actually really proud of that guitar solo.

GW: Do you use any open tunings when you play slide?

HAMMETT: Man, that shit just confuses me. When I found out that Duane Allman used standard tuning, it really inspired me to work on my slide chops. Before that, I thought that slide players all worked in open G and could use all the tricky tunings.

GW: The solo on "Bleeding Me" also sounds particularly inspired.

HAMMETT: That's the one lead that I played totally off-the-cuff. I did seven or eight passes, and it felt so goddamn good. Every time I finished a take, Bob would look at me and say, "Wow!" It's one of the more typical "rock" solos on the album. I had the wah pedal going, and I was going for a combination of fast playing and long, sustained notes. It has everything in there: melody, hooks, rock and roll phrasing, a bluesy vibe, lots of dynamics, and the Hendrixisms that I always try to sneak in there.

GW: James, you also play quite a bit of lead guitar on *Load*.

HETFIELD: Honest to goodness, I don't know anymore. So much different shit has gone on this record as far as laying guitar tracks that I kind of forget what actually made it into the final mix.

HAMMETT: I don't feel as possessive about the guitar parts as I have in the past, precisely because there's so much there. I mean, ultimately it doesn't really matter who played what; the parts are just there to make the songs happen. I mean at this point, I think that people know we can play.

GW: All of *Load* is tuned down a half step—another first for you.

HETFIELD: Tuning down a half step helped a lot of things, like getting the bends going in the riffs. The most fun thing in the world is sitting down with your guitar tuned down a whole step and riffing out. Unfortunately, that sounds too muddy, so we settled for tuning down a half step. Tuning down also helps me a lot by extending the apparent range of my voice.

GW: Vocally, you've taken a lot of chances with this album.

HETFIELD: I feel that it's more raw. It was a lot more fun doing the vocals this time, not as stiff a process. We were trying to be a little less anal.

GW: In the past, though, Metallica has always been a band that holds itself to an extreme level of studio perfection.

HETFIELD: There's still that. There's still a desire for perfection, but this time we let little things go. If the verdict was, "Well, that thing you sang was a bit pitchy, but it has some major attitude," then fuck it, let it ride.

On *Metallica*, the vocals were so in the pocket all the time. I was trapped by the fact that I forced myself to repeat certain phrases exactly every time they occurred within a song.

GW: Did you go so far as to use vocal sampling on the last album, to ensure that recurring parts would be exactly the same?

HETFIELD: Well, there were a couple of times where we flew in the background vocals on a chorus or something—just to save the time doing the donkey work. But I didn't feel right about doing even that this time. I sang everything.

GW: On "Poor Twisted Me," your vocals are distorted. Is there an industrial music influence creeping in there?

HETFIELD: We wanted to get some different sounds. That's just a good old Shure bullet mic, usually used for harmonica. It's got a distinct sound that you can't do too much to, but it's pretty cool for what it is.

But I wouldn't call that an industrial sound or anything. It's just a mic being used for an application it wasn't designed for. The song called out for it. I had always told myself, "I'm never ever going to use that distorted vocal sound that everyone uses." But it fit lyrically.

I've been really focusing on lyricists—as opposed to people who just sit down and crank out some words for a song—who write fucking poems and then put music to them. I wanted to understand other people's ideas about how to write lyrics. Nick Cave's *Murder Ballads* are the coolest, and I dig all the Tom Waits stuff. I've even listened to some Leonard Cohen. I mean, I hate the fucking music, but his lyrics are very cool.

GW: You do a lot more "acting" with your singing.

HETFIELD: The way we recorded the vocals this time made it a bit easier, not exactly to get into character, but to feel the vocals a bit more than before. All the other times I did vocals, I sat in front of some expensive microphone—stranded out in the cold fucking tracking room. There always was a big X on the floor, and I wasn't allowed to move from that spot.

This time I thought, "You know, I have a great time with the vocals in my studio at home. I fuck around with them and they come out fine. Why can't we try that here?" So we'd take the SM-57 or whatever mic we were using and I would walk around the control room and just yell—and it was fine. It was very liberating not having to worry about where I had to stand and all this other bullshit. I could just worry about what I was singing.

GW: Apparently, Henry Rollins does much the same thing when he's cutting vocals. He actually has to tape the headphones to his head because he gets so animated.

HETFIELD: Fuck headphones, man! We had the big fatties [*large studio monitors*] cranked. There's a little bleed, but fuck it. You've got to go for vibe.

GW: Earlier you referred to "a lot of changes happening in Metallica." What, besides the changes in your rhythm guitar approach—and your haircuts—were you referring to?

HETFIELD: In general, there's a looser attitude. Some new things happened with Jason [*Newsted, bassist*]. In the past, Lars [*Ulrich, drummer*] and I had the fucking shackles on everybody. This time, if we came into the studio and heard Jason laying down some slap bass part on a song, we'd be like, "What the fuck? Okay, let's count to 10 and hear it in the context of the song. We're open-minded here." It was difficult at times.

I had noticed over the years how frustrated Jason was musically and how a lot of the stuff he'd written wasn't getting onto the records. It also used to really bug me that he was jamming with all of these other bands. He'd make a demo with some friends, and somehow it would end up on the radio, and I'd be like, "What the fuck are you doing, Jason? This is Metallica! You can't do that shit!" Then I realized that he was doing it because he needs to get his shit out. He wants people to hear his stuff.

HAMMETT: It's a good creative outlet and completely healthy for him. And ultimately, what's healthy for him is healthy for us.

HETFIELD: We kept his frustration in mind while we hashed out the parts he put down on the record.

GW: Are there specific things on *Metallica* that you wanted to improve on *Load*?

HAMMETT: The one thing that strikes me about *Metallica* when I go back and listen to it is that there isn't enough variation in my tone. I kind of stuck with the same sound, and the only variation was a wah pedal here and a wah pedal there, or the minimal tonal variation that you get from tuning down.

But you can't really look back. If you do, you end up constantly comparing yourself to the past, and that has a way of holding you back. You end up with a whole catalog of albums that sound like one particular album that was successful. The idea should be to move forward and try and develop a new vision.

GW: You did, however, keep one important part of the *Metallica* formula intact when you decided to work with Bob Rock again. How has your relationship with him developed?

HETFIELD: When we started working on *Metallica*, Bob was much more passive than he is now. He was afraid to take control. Now our relationship goes through phases, depending on what needs to be done. At different times, Bob tries to exert a little more authority over us. We laugh at him and move on. [*laughs*]

HAMMETT: The thing with Bob is that he can read us pretty well at this point—he definitely knows what we're capable of. I know that on this album I came in and did a really great job at what I had to do, and a lot of that was the result of him zoning on a particular idea that I had and him telling me to build on it. Then there have been times where I've been a bit hung over and not happening, and he's flown off the handle and yelled, "Get your shit together!"

But you know what—and I probably shouldn't say this—there have been times when I've come in hung over and been able to play really well. And I think that in a few of those situations, being hung over has added a certain edge to my playing.

HETFIELD: [*laughs*] Oh no!

HAMMETT: I'm not advocating drinking, and this is a highly personal point of view, but there has been the occasional session where I've come in a little hung over—not super hung over—and it's made me think more and feel a little more sensitive to the needs of the track.

HETFIELD: Kids, don't try this at home.

HAMMETT: But getting back to Bob, I think that he's really good at coaching us through things.

HETFIELD: That's his gig. He's not here to tell us what to do. He's trying to get the best shit he can out of us all the time.

He's also a really solid guitar player with a good knowledge of theory, which can be really helpful in a bind. I'll be trying to work out a harmony, and he'll come in and say, "Well, A is the relative minor of blah blah blah," and since I don't know any of that shit, it's nice to have the instruction booklet right next to me.

HAMMETT: He's always pulling out the relative minor. It's his favorite thing.

GW: *Load* has much more of an in-your-face mix than *Metallica*, which had considerable amounts of ambiance in the mix.

HETFIELD: I wanted the guitars back in your face again. I like the way *Kill 'Em All* (1983) just had fucking guitars up your ass and the drums were not the leader of the group. I think that on the "Black Album," everyone wanted to be up front. But something has to be back there, and it ended up being the guitars, which were given a wider, thinner sound and pushed back. I think that on this album, the drums drive the rhythm instead of leading the band, and there are these two guitars playing different things right up front.

I had one big fear when we went to the two guitar player thing: "Is the fucking riff still going to be heard?" That's always been really important in this group. But I think we found a nice balance between them, and their level in the mix was crucial.

GW: Were you asked to play Lollapalooza? Or did you do the asking?

HETFIELD: They asked us. We thought about it and said, "All right, why the fuck not?" All it is is a European style rock festival. We've done festivals all over the world.

HAMMETT: It's like the Reading Festival [*an annual British festival*]— except that it moves from place to place. We're used to being on different bills with different people. I mean, we played one festival in Belgium where we shared the bill with Neil Young, Lenny Kravitz, Sugar, Sonic Youth, the Levelers and the Black Crowes. That would never happen in America because those bands mean something completely different over here than they do in Europe.

The whole impetus behind Lollapalooza was to do something different and challenging. And I think that the bill with us on it is different and challenging more recently, they were stuck in a rut where they had to have alternative bands and indie bands.

GW: Is it true that you played an important role in selecting the bands for this year's line-up?

HAMMETT: We did and we didn't. A lot of it had to do with availability. A lot of bands that we wanted were touring on their own. I mean, I would have liked to have Al Green or the Cocteau Twins.

HETFIELD: We're not picking Lollapalooza. We're not coming in to take it over. We're just gonna play. We don't really want to have anything to do with Lollapalooza except play it.

GW: Are you looking forward to seeing any of the bands that will be on the bill with you.

HAMMETT: I like the vibe of Lollapalooza. I've been to every single one; I've actually jammed at a few, too. When Ministry was out I played with them a few times, and I did the same with Primus. I've fucking loved Soundgarden since '85 or '86. And everyone loves the Ramones. I was talking to Johnny Ramone the other day, and he was saying, "Goddamn it Kirk, I'd already be retired and playing golf in L.A. if it wasn't for you guys calling us up and asking us to do this summer tour." And I said, "Well Johnny, there isn't any better way to go."

GUITAR WORLD, JULY 1996

BASS DESIRES

Metallica's quiet man discovers his voice.
By Tom Beaujour

I N THE DECADE since bassist Jason Newsted joined Metallica, the group has toured the world, produced three stellar albums and ascended to the upper stratum of rock stardom. But even as Newsted gained great satisfaction from the band's success, he often felt frustrated within Metallica's well-defined musical hierarchy, one in which James Hetfield and Kirk Hammett hold a riff-writing monopoly. "James writes the best metal songs on the planet. He has proved it time and time again. Kirk comes up with great shit too, and between the two of them, they're pretty much unbeatable," Newsted explains.

Resigned to the likelihood that his songwriting skills would probably always be underutilized within Metallica's confines, Newsted embarked on a series of side projects, one of which, IR8, landed him in a world of trouble.

"A while back, I did a side project, called IR8, with Devon Townshend [*ex-Steve Vai band*] and Tom Hunting, the original drummer from Exodus," says Newsted. "I gave one tape to this guy in L.A. and one to a guy in Ohio. By the next afternoon, it was being played on KNAC [*a popular Los Angeles hard rock radio station*] and a few other stations. The tape spread like wildfire. A couple of weeks later, we were getting fan mail from Greece and Turkey.

"Metallica called a meeting to discuss the situation, and I said, 'Look, man, I'm sorry if this got out of hand, but I had to express myself. I'm writing this gnarly-as-fuck new school of metal shit. I would never want to do anything to make Metallica look bad or less than it is, but the outside musical projects that I do help keep Metallica fresh for me.' "

After the fateful meeting, Newsted was granted considerably more creative control. "Everything changed," he says. "They realized that everyone in this band is a thinking, creative person who has something to say."

GUITAR WORLD: Do you have free reign when it comes to writing the bass lines, or do James and Kirk get involved?

JASON NEWSTED: This time, there was no one breathing down my neck, no one pointing fingers, saying, "play this, play that," although that kind of thing had taken place in some form or other on the previous albums. This time [*producer*] Bob Rock, [*engineer*] Randy Staub and myself were the only people around. It was like, "We are the bass team, we are putting the bass on the fucking new Metallica album, and that's all there is to it. When it comes to Metallica, I have one job: to go in there with my bass line and make the song greater."

GW: Do you write a lot of material to submit to Metallica?

NEWSTED: I came in with 25 songs for *Load*, some of which we recorded basic tracks for, but I don't think that any of that material will be on this album. If I get songwriting credit because a bass part I came up with took a song in a whole new direction, then fine. But it's not an issue that I'm sweating anymore. I'm through chewing myself up. I simply want to be the best bass player that I can be for this band.

GW: You seem to have remained plugged in to the current metal scene more than the other members of Metallica. Are there any groups in particular that you're jazzed about?

NEWSTED: I really dig Fear Factory, Machine Head and especially Sepultura. Their new album, *Roots* (Roadrunner), is devastating.

GW: Does it bother you that hard metal is not represented in the

Lollapalooza line-up?

NEWSTED: When the Lollapalooza thing came up, they asked us to suggest bands for the second and third stages, so each of us wrote our own little lists. Mine included Voivod, Sepultura and Machine Head. I just wanted to get a little flavor in there.

Unfortunately, when I bring up the heavy bands at meetings, it doesn't go over too well anymore. The rest of the guys are sort of in a different place than I am as far as heavy music goes. Their feet are still firmly planted in the New Wave of British Heavy Metal and Sabbath, but they've moved on to more melodic rock and pop music.

GW: Despite the absence on the tour of the bands on your wish list, are you still looking forward to Lollapalooza?

NEWSTED: Oh, totally. I've got big plans for the tour, inspired by a project of [*King Crimson and session bassist*] Tony Levin.

When he was touring around the world with Peter Gabriel and the likes, Tony, using an ADAT as well as some local studios, recorded himself jamming with all these different cats, none of whom could speak English. He jammed with reed players, banjo guys, people who invented their own instruments—you name it. Then he brought all the tapes home, layered on more tracks and made a record called *World Diary* (Papa Bear).

For the Lollapalooza tour, I'm going to have my own tour bus and do my own version of Tony's thing. There are going to be so many people playing at Lollapalooza, especially when you take into account all the bands that latch onto the tour for a handful of dates. I hope to find these people any time of the fucking day or night and have them come onto my bus, or go into a field or a tent, and record them in different combinations.

For the past six months, I've been designing a portable setup around the Roland VG-8 and the new Roland VS-880 eight-track digital recorder, and I've got it down to two suitcases. While I'm out on the road, I just want to get the cleanest signals I possibly can. When I get the stuff home, I'll put on some effects and make a huge sick broth of gnarly sounds. If this works on Lollapalooza, then I'll take it around the world.

GUITAR WORLD, OCTOBER 1991

SKULLDUGGERY

A look at the bewildering, ever-growing field of Metallica artifacts and memorabilia.

By K.J. Doughton

IT HAPPENS TO every rock memorabilia collector. You slave over fan magazine classifieds, hang out at merchandise stands and hound local radio stations, all in an effort to increase your heap of collectibles. Though you've singled out only one band, the quest becomes difficult. Things begin slipping through your greedy, rarity-clutching fingers. For all your T-shirts, posters, cardboard standups, limited-edition singles, fan club biographies and logo-emblazoned demo tapes, you hang your head in despair. You can't keep up.

The Metallica collector is particularly susceptible to the melancholic hazards of his avocation, as the sheer extent of the material associated with the band is in itself cause for despair. Only the people at Brocum are truly happy, as Metallica is the merchandising concern's best-selling client—quite a distinction, considering that the company also handles rock giants like Guns N' Roses and the Scorpions.

Just as Iron Maiden T-shirts could be seen adorning teenage torsos on street corners across the U.S. five years ago, Metallica tees are today's rocking garment-of-choice. And like Iron Maiden, whose skeletal mascot, Eddie, became more recognizable than any of the band members, Metallica has a soft spot for skulls, bones and reaper-ish visions of death-in-life.

The man responsible for the memorably ghoulish symbols is Pushead, who first encountered the band in 1985. The San Francisco area illustrator's maiden Metallica assignment was to design the "Damage, Inc." tour shirt. His creation—a skull impaled by two spiked clubs—was a great success. The shirts sold by the truckload, in the process resurrecting the skeletal imagery that is now the sta-ple of rock paraphernalia.

The artist has made such a mark on Metallica's image that we've divided this merchandise outline into "Before Pushead" and "After Pushead" sections. Following the endless list of Metalli-knicknacks can be both fun and frustrating. In preparing this information, I con-tacted Pushead and tapped into his encyclopedic familiarity with Metallica merchandise. The Metallica art-man rattled off over 20 band artifacts that I never even knew existed. "If you're a serious Metallica collector," said Pushead, with a ghastly grin, "I've just made your life a nightmare." Thank God for mild sedatives.

BEFORE PUSHEAD T-SHIRTS

The first "official" Metallica T-shirt displayed the band logo, with the slogan "The Young Metal Attack" inscribed underneath. Only a handful were printed during the band's pre-*Kill 'Em All* days in Los Angeles. Nearly impossible to find now, it was followed by the Metallica "Metal Up Your Ass" shirt. Not to be confused with Brocum's popular "machete-through-toilet" design, this ultra-rare version featured the group logo and a sparse "Metal Up Your Ass" etched beneath. Another pre-Brocum Metallica garment worth seek-ing out is the "Kill 'Em All for One" tour shirt, sold during the land-mark 1983 cross-country tour co-headlined by Metallica and the band's UK labelmates, Raven.

DEMOS AND BOOTLEGS

Tons of Metallica demos and bootlegs are floating about on tape. The real task is finding a collector who can dub off the early recordings.

Try the classified ad sections of the more popular metal magazines. The "must have" tapes include *No Life 'Til Leather* (1982), essentially a demo tape of most of the material from the first Metallica album. Extra points go to those who find the demo's original cover sleeve, drawn by James Hetfield and including a song listing, band logo, etc. *Live Metal Up Your Ass* (11/29/82) immortalized the band's last live gig with bassist Ron McGovney, and also features a Hetfield-stenciled cover that is very tough to find.

A pre-*Kill 'Em All* demo of "Whiplash" and "No Remorse" (2/83) is also worth tracking down, as is a pre-*Ride the Lightning* demo (12/83) that is notable for its inclusion of "When Hell Freezes Over," which, renamed "Call Of Ktulu," wound up on *Ride the Lighting*. Digging deeper, one might also keep a sharp eye out for what allegedly was the band's *Metal Massacre* demo tape (1981), which includes enthusiastic-yet-primitive versions of two New Wave of British Heavy Metal songs as well as Metallica's first version of "Hit the Lights."

Pre-Metallica Cliff Burton can be heard on the demo tape by the band Trauma, "Shame a Shame" (1982). Kirk Hammett shows up on a 1982 Exodus demo tape recorded during his time with that band. Meanwhile, there are literally thousands of live Metallica bootlegs on tape and record. The vinyl releases are, of course, unauthorized, but such lavishly packaged discs as *Horsemen of the Apokalypse*, *Fucking Nuts* and *The Final Gig* (one of many Cliff Burton dedication bootlegs) are definitely worth checking out. Severely misspelled song titles on the sleeve notes are good for a laugh.

VINYL

Like most metal acts, Metallica has a massive vinyl output that reflects a desire to please the fanatical collector by offering special-edition discs and exclusive B-side tracks. Their *Creeping Death* 12-inch EP (Music for Nations, 1985) is a good example, with its "Am I Evil" and "Blitzkrieg" B-side cover tracks. Speaking of *Creeping Death*, the EP was released in black, blue, green, clear, gold and mixed vinyl versions. Once you've uncovered those, track down the picture-disc version as well. Other interesting EPs include Megaforce's *Whiplash* single (1985) and Music for Nations' *Jump in the Fire* record (1984), which includes a live B-side and can also be found in "shaped disc" form.

As far as albums go, one would be wise to snag a copy of the original Megaforce version of *Kill 'Em All*, as it is no longer in print (only Elektra releases the album at this time). The tell-tale difference between the Megaforce and Elektra versions is that the Elektra includes two extra tracks ("Blitzkrieg" and "Am I Evil?," from the "Creeping Death" B-side). Also, the first French pressing of *Ride the Lightning* was mistakenly released with uncharacteristically green cover artwork, due to a printing error (which some cynics maintain was actually an intentional maneuver, designed to bolster French album sales). It's not an easy catch. On the first pressing of Megaforce's U.S. version of *Ride*, there's a spelling error on the sleeve—instead of the proper "For Whom the Bell Tolls," it reads "For Whom the Bells Toll."

The band's third album, *Master of Puppets*, was released as a special-edition double album with gatefold sleeve, poster and stickers (Music for Nations, 1986). In addition, the U.S. promotional version of *Master* was fastened with an amusing sticker which parodied the Tipper Gore-inspired album obscenity warning: "The only track you probably don't want to play is 'Damage, Inc.,' due to multiple use of the infamous 'F' word. Otherwise, there aren't any 'shits,' 'fucks,' 'pisses,' 'cunts,' 'motherfuckers' or 'cocksuckers' anywhere on this record." Unoffended collectors might be on the lookout for a copy. Meanwhile, all of Metallica's early albums can be found in picture-disc form, as well.

Other early vinyl treasures include the glow-in-the-dark "Fade to Black" 12-inch promo single (Elektra, 1985), and such radio promo EPs as *For Whom the Bell Tolls* and *Master of Puppets*. Perhaps the hardest single to find is the "Master of Puppets" French 7-inch promo (Music for Nations/N.E.W., 1986), complete with cover-sleeve.

AFTER PUSHEAD T-SHIRTS
Pushead's skeleton artwork adorns everything from skateboards to

jewelry; he's even putting the finishing touches on a trading card collection. But T-shirts are his forte. The acclaimed artist's "Eye of the Beholder" design (originally drawn as cover art for the band's single but also appearing on tour shirts) eerily collages four eyes to create an unsettling effect. "I took photos of the four Metallica members' eyes," explains Pushead, "and then I drew the design from the photos."

Another provocative shirt features artwork for the band's "One" single. Maintaining the "living vegetable" imagery, the design depicts a bandaged carcass with bloody limbs and a skull-face swinging from the strings of a parachute.

"My idea for 'One' was that he was on display," says the illustrator. "That's why he's pictured in a corner. Then there's the sick humor of it—he has no limbs, his brain is exposed, he's swinging himself back and forth, and the blood spells 'Metallica.' It's kind of like in the movie *Johnny Got His Gun* [*which inspired the song and video*], where the guy blinked his eyes in Morse code because it was the only way he could communicate. It's one of those drawings where people either think it's really sick or kind of cute."

While dozens of other official Pushead shirts are marketed under Brocum's sizable merchandise umbrella, there are a few "freaks" out there, too—special designs produced for the band and tour crew alone. "Captains of Krunch," for instance, parodies Captain Crunch with a design depicting Metallica on a cereal box. Collectors take note—it's unavailable via retail.

JAPANESE ITEMS

An explosion of Japanese Metallica items has expanded the merchandise frontier even wider. CBS/Sony, the band's Far East record label, recently released the group's *2 of One* video on 8-inch laser disc. Additionally, rare posters are emerging from Japan—two that feature Pushead's artwork, one showing a spider, the other Mount Fuji, are particular favorites. However, the most sought-after Japanese artifact is a metal painter's can embossed with the Metallica logo that comes with a T-shirt and CD inside. Only 6,000 exist, so look carefully.

OTHER ITEMS

Every self-respecting Metallica fan must own the *5.98 EP: Garage Days Re-Revisited*, *...And Justice for All*, and the many readily available singles that came out with the latter album's release. It should go without saying that the *Cliff 'Em All* and *2 of One* videos are Metallica staples of major merit. Among the overwhelming tide of Metallica calendars, songbooks, tour books and posters too numerous to list here, a few currently-sought-after trinkets should be noted. The *Stone Cold Crazy* promo CD (Elektra, 1991) is certainly a worthy trophy, as is the Elektra-issued, Metallica-inscribed marble paperweight. The most exciting piece of Metalli-memorabilia to surface in quite some time, however, is the multi-CD box set *The Good, the Bad, and the Live*, comprised of all the band's singles, B-side material, the *5.98 EP* and previously unreleased live performances from the "Damaged Justice" tour. Available nationwide, it ought to be more than enough to satiate collectors as they assemble the other pieces of the never-ending Metallica merchandise puzzle.

GUITAR WORLD, OCTOBER 1992

KIRK HAMMETT: WHY I PLAY GUITAR

As told to Harold Steinblatt

"WHEN I WAS growing up in San Francisco during the Seventies, I used to hang around with my brother and his college friends. When my family moved to a small suburb, he stayed in the city. I missed him a lot, and to fill the void, I listened to a lot of the same music he would listen to: Hendrix, Zeppelin, Cream, Deep Purple and Santana. After that, I learned that a friend of mine was selling an electric guitar, and I got it. My brother also played, so I asked for his approval to start playing.

"For a couple of months, I just fooled around on the guitar for half an hour or so and then set it back down in my closet. When I visited my brother in the city, he asked me if I was still playing guitar. I didn't want to tell him that I wasn't, so I said yes. He said that was great, and then suggested that we go and get some new strings for my guitar. So we went and got 'em—for five bucks of my hard-earned money—and restrung my guitar, and that's when I really started playing.

"I started buying instructional books, but they just didn't teach what I wanted to know. So, I started listening to albums to learn. I never had much of a social life in high school, and was always kind of shy and introverted. And I never really had anything to do. So I started playing like crazy. Plus, since I idolized some of the great players so much, once I started learning their music, I felt closer to them as people. I felt I could understand them better, and that we had some sort of a spiritual relationship.

"Michael Schenker played a major role in shaping my style, and I finally got to meet him last year. I immediately told him how I learned everything he did while he was in UFO and MSG, and how I tried to get his sound by buying a Flying V, Marshalls and wah pedals. And I started to spazz out—my girlfriend had to kick me and tell me to calm down. In a weird way, to me it was like meeting Santa Claus—that's how much of an impact he had on me.

"I finally felt comfortable with my improvisation and what I was creating about three or four years into my playing. I realized that musical ideas are like seeds, and that ideas grow from other ideas. I started to see the guitar as a blank canvas, and myself as a painter. I was on to something that was creatively satisfying to me. Before then, I was always a daydreamer. The guitar was very fulfilling because it enabled me to express my daydreams musically.

"When I was younger, I thought that what I was playing was really great, and I went with that gunslinger attitude for a while. But now I realize that, back then, I was very frustrated because I hadn't reached the playing plateau that I wanted to reach. I recently realized that I've already been at that plateau for a few years, and now I've set new goals for myself—mostly in terms of being able to express myself in different ways. I'm learning the blues now like I never have before, and I'm listening to players like Albert King and Buddy Guy—guys who influenced the players who influenced me when I was younger—sort of traveling up the musical family tree.

"I feel like I've finally reached the goal that I set for myself when I was 13 or 14: to be able to play very coherently, and to say things on my guitar that I wasn't able to in normal conversation. I feel much more mature in my relationship with my instrument. Nowadays, whenever I learn something new or write something good, I feel like I've just made a deposit in the bank of creative ideas."

GUITAR WORLD, OCTOBER 1991

METALLICA ACOUSTICA

James Hetfield and Kirk Hammett demonstrate that real men thrash electrically—and sometimes acoustically.
By Brad Tolinski

"WE WERE SEARCHING for a new clarity," says James Hetfield in his deliberate, surprisingly mellow baritone voice. "Each instrument had to be heard distinctly. I recorded maybe two or three guitars for each rhythm part, instead of my usual eight or nine. We wanted everything to be punchy and right in your face."

To achieve this new milestone in heaviness on *Metallica*, Hetfield and his fellow high priest of thrash, Kirk Hammett, used ESP—guitars, that is. "I used an ESP Strat for 80 percent of the record," Hammett says. "It has a real bite, which is what I look for; I don't like the high-end sizzle I hear on a lot of new guitars. I've always felt that a guitar tone should simply be an amplification of the guitar's acoustic qualities—and I don't hear that sizzle when I'm not plugged in."

Hetfield's primary axe on *Metallica* was an ESP Explorer. The guitar resembles the classic Gibson Explorer in shape, but the similarities end there. "It's made of a denser wood, for better tone," explains Hetfield. "Also, the neck is less 'loggy' and is flatter than the standard Gibson model."

Both Hetfield and Hammett's ESPs are equipped with EMG

pickups. "The reason I use EMGs is simple: low noise and high output," says Hammett. "We boost both low and high frequencies pretty radically—our sound is pretty scooped at both ends of the spectrum—and for those drastic EQs, EMGs work the best. The lows they generate are very warm sounding. In general, the pickups are very versatile. For example, my neck position EMG on my '89 Gibson Les Paul Deluxe has a wonderful sound."

"I started using EMGs on the *Ride the Lightning* tour," adds Hetfield. "They attracted me because of their tight low-end. I have them installed in a really weird way—I think they're in backwards, which is probably why my sound is so unique." [*laughs*]

Hetfield colored his tone with the help of several guitars he selected from producer Bob Rock's extensive collection. "We tried to get some unique clean sounds on *Metallica*, so we experimented with a few guitars," Hetfield says. "I used a Gretsch White Falcon for that descending effect at the end of the chorus on 'Nothing Else Matters.' I tried it in several other places, but it was a little too twangy for my taste. I also used an old Telecaster for that distant, *The Good, the Bad and the Ugly* opening melody in 'The Unforgiven.' "

To the casual listener, the ballad "Nothing Else Matters" sounds as if it were performed on an acoustic instrument. Not so, says Hetfield: "Most of that song was played on a Tom Anderson electric guitar. We recorded it using two extremely clean signals: one through an amp and the other directly into the board. We really worked hard on that sound, and are real proud of the results. We also used a jumbo Guild acoustic 12-string on the choruses. To get a fuller sound, we tuned the 12-string's high E-string down to a D."

Hetfield's other acoustic guitars include an Aria nylon-string (a gift from Cliff Burton, the Metallica bassist who died in 1986) and a Fender Shenandoah steel-string. Both are featured on "The Unforgiven." The Shenandoah was used for its "shimmery, high-end qualities."

To Hetfield, the most difficult aspect of recording acoustics was finding an instrument that was properly balanced. "We went through a lot of guitars," he says. "We'd bring in some beautiful

$20,000 guitar, mic it up, and find that some of the strings were louder than the others. You can only compress an acoustic guitar so much before it starts sounding pinched.

"We don't yet know whether we're going to play acoustic on stage. We'd like to, but sometimes it doesn't work too well. We tried to play acoustically once, but someone in the audience threw something and knocked all the guitars over. We haven't tried it since," Hetfield laughs.

For amplification, lead guitarist Hammett found that a combination of two Marshalls, in conjunction with a Bradshaw preamp, a VHT power amp and 30-watt Celestion speakers, delivered the sweet, yet piercing sound he was searching for. "I'm not sure what year either Marshall is," Hammett says. "One was an old purple 100-watt Super Lead, and the other was a 50-watt head. The Bradshaw worked great in the studio because it really helped blend the different amp sounds. I didn't use my Mesa/Boogie Simul-class II amp in the studio this time out, because James was using it in his setup and we didn't want to disassemble it."

Hetfield produced his patented crunch compliments of Hammett's Mesa/Boogie II. "I've been looking for extras, but they're pretty difficult to get a hold of," remarks Hetfield.

No discussion of Metallica's equipment would be complete without a brief seminar on the uses and true meaning of the wah-wah pedal, conducted by its leading modern-day exponent, Kirk Hammett:

"I use a late-Sixties Vox wah pedal that is rumored to have once belonged to Jimi Hendrix. It makes my guitar sound jump out of the mix, and brings out the best aspects of my playing.

"I was really influenced and inspired by Hendrix's basic approach on *Electric Ladyland* and *Cry of Love*. But it wasn't just Hendrix; Pat Travers and Thin Lizzy's Brian Robertson also left a tremendous impact on my approach to playing wah-wah. In fact, I think I learned every single note off of Pat's live album; it really helped shape my playing and phrasing."

A final important element of the Metallica sonic arsenal is also extremely inexpensive: the simple process of detuning.

"You can just tell when a riff needs to be tuned down," asserts Hetfield. "For example, 'The God That Failed' just begged to be detuned a half step, for that added heaviness. 'Sad but True' is tuned down a whole step, but that's about as far as we'll go. When you go down that low, it becomes difficult to stay in tune. We used to play 'The Thing That Should Not Be' live, and detune two whole steps! That's pretty far down there. Our strings were flapping in the breeze! Man, we'd listen to live tapes—and whoa—we'd be way out of tune!"

Jay Blakesberg

GUITAR WORLD, JULY 1996

HEAVY DUTY

The gear behind LOAD's crushing sound.
By Tom Beaujour

"GETTING MY RHYTHM guitar sound is always the most nerve-wracking part of the recording process for me," says James Hetfield. "Once that's done, it's pretty much clear sailing as far as I'm concerned." To deliver the lion's share of *Load*'s ear-punishing crunch, Hetfield called upon his trusty white ESP Explorer, loaded with EMG 81 pickups. "It's pretty much the first one they made for me, and it's just the shit," he says. "For some reason, it just sounds better than the others. That guitar doesn't travel—I save it for studio work."

The guitarist's main amplifier setup was composed of a Jose Arrendondo-modified Marshall, a Mesa/Boogie Tri-Axis preamp and a Mesa/Boogie C+ that he " 'borrowed' from Kirk years ago. That amp always comes through in the studio."

To achieve some of the album's subtler textures, Hetfield used a variety of other guitars, among them a B-bender-equipped '52 reissue Telecaster, a Gretsch White Falcon and a '63 Gibson SG that was a birthday gift from producer Bob Rock. "It was an especially cool gift because I was born in '63," Hetfield explains. "Now I'm waiting for a '63 Strat. Maybe next album."

Also on hand were a veritable battery of amps, all of which

were put to good use. "At one point, I had 14 amps going at once...for a clean sound," says Hetfield. "I wanted to get a variety of clean sounds on this album instead of relying exclusively on the Roland JC-120, which has traditionally been the source of Metallica's clean sound. It was tough going, though, because the Roland sounds so good that you want to keep going back to it. But we found some other cool amps, particularly this little Matchless Spitfire that really kicks ass and an old tweed Fender Twin that's so sharp it'll take your nuts off!"

To contrast with the high, full-throttle grind of Hetfield's EMG-equipped Explorer, Kirk Hammett found himself relying heavily on the vintage virtues of a PAF-loaded '58 Les Paul Standard. "PAFs have a warmth and clarity that you just can't get from new guitars," Hammett says. "That guitar sounded so completely different from James' that I was able to plug directly into his setup without making too many changes, expect maybe putting a Tube Screamer in front or adding a little Matchless Spitfire or Vox AC30 to the mix. For some of the cleaner rhythm parts, I also used my '64 seafoam-green Strat, which provided an even greater contrast to James' Explorer."

For his lead work, Hammett made use of the two aforementioned vintage jewels, as well as several other instruments from his mouth-watering guitar collection. "The slide solo on 'Ain't My Bitch' was done with a '62 or '63 Les Paul Junior that was set up with high action and sounded phenomenal. Some other slide work was done on a '63 Gibson ES-335 and on the '58 Les Paul. I also used my '58 Flying V on a couple of tracks. What can I say? Old guitars just sound better," concludes Hammett, who wishes it to be known that all of the guitars in his collection are used and abused on a regular basis. "I don't believe in guitars being display pieces," he says.

The guitarist, who also made a few concessions to the virtues of modern guitar-making by using an '88 Les Paul and several of his ESP Signature models, was particularly enamored of the endless tonal possibilities supplied by the Roland VG-8 effects unit. The VG-8 can be heard on several of *Load*'s tracks, in particular the ethereal

"F.O.B.D." "I think the VG-8 is one of the best inventions ever," Hammett effuses. "If you get tired of one sound, you can just switch presets and explore entirely new possibilities. I've spent hours fucking around with it."

Jason Newsted's quest for the perfect bass sound was relatively painless—this time. "It was much easier to get a sound on *Load* because we had gone through everything imaginable to get the sound on the 'Black Album,' " he says. "We ended up going back to the same basses that I always use, a Spector and a '58 Fender Precision Bass that I played on 'The Unforgiven,' on the last album. On this record, we discovered how truly fantastic that bass really is. My basic sound is the P-bass straight into a solid-state Ampeg Portaflex B-15." A few Mesa/Boogie amps were also on hand.

"We did a lot more experimenting with effects this time," Newsted continues. "There's an Electro-Harmonix Big Muff on 10 of the 14 songs. Other Electro-Harmonix pedals we recorded with were the Dr. Q envelope filter and Small Stone phaser, and we also used an MXR Microsynth and a Korg Hyperbass processor." Newsted plans to use Music Man Stingray basses on tour.

GUITAR WORLD, OCTOBER 1991

FIGHT FIRE WITH FIRE

Kirk Hammett demonstrates the sophisticated techniques with which he counterpoints the sheer power of his partner in thrash, James Hetfield.
By Wolf Marshall

KIRK HAMMETT, ONE OF thrash's most compelling guitarists, boasts an instantly recognizable, eclectic style that is the product of a melting pot of influences. The recipe for guitar à la Kirk includes some tasty blues-rock morsels of Hendrix, Page, Clapton and Beck, a liberal dash of Joe Perry and Pat Travers and generous helpings of Euro-metal via Michael Schenker and Uli Roth. Add a significant amount of technical training and theoretical insight from the maestro Satriani to this mixture, and you begin to get an idea of what Kirk Hammett is all about.

But beyond ingredients and playing experience, there remains the phenomenon of Hammett—making it all work within the teeming context of Metallica, one of the most musically sophisticated and unpredictable bands in the complex world of speed metal. What does he do? How does he do it? These were the very questions Hammett and I set out to answer.

James Hetfield, referring to the diabolical harmonic twists and turns of Metallica's music, once joked of his partner's plight as chief soloist, "Sometimes, with the chords I throw at him, he doesn't know what to play. I mean, who would? He has to make up new scales—or forget old ones!" Hammett certainly has his job cut out for him—creating meaningful and interesting solo lines to complement Hetfield's odd, often dissonant, chord progressions. A good case in point is shown in **Figure 1**, similar to what Hammett plays in his live "Ride the Lightning" solo.

FIGURE 1

As Hetfield lays down the chromatically descending power chord progression, C5-B5-Bb5-A5, Hammett's melody takes on a life of its own. The solo and chords are independent of each other, yet interlocking—the essence of melodic/harmonic interaction. Here's how it works. As Hetfield pounds out the power chords, Hammett plays a series of triad arpeggios (indicated in parentheses) in a steady 16th-note rhythm, employing a common-tone principle well-known to jazz guitarists. The common tones fall on the second 16th note of each beat (the third of each triad) and correspond to the root notes of the underlying power chords. For example, in the first bar, Hammett plays an A minor arpeggio (A, C, E) over Hetfield's C5 chord (C, G). The common tone in this case is C. Note that he uses the same fretboard shape for the Am, Gm and F#m arpeggios. "The pattern follows the chords down with arpeggios," Hammett explains. "I think I got the G major thing by accident! I play the whole lick on the first and second strings and mostly use downstrokes."

Figure 2, similar to a lick from Hammett's solo in "One," shows him soloing over Hetfield's E5-F5 changes (Em Phrygian progression) with a sequence of two-hand taps. Note the triads outlined: E minor, C major, B minor (not indigenous to the E Phrygian mode) and G major. (Randy Rhoads used a similar arpeggio sequence in his "Crazy Train" solo.)

FIGURE 2

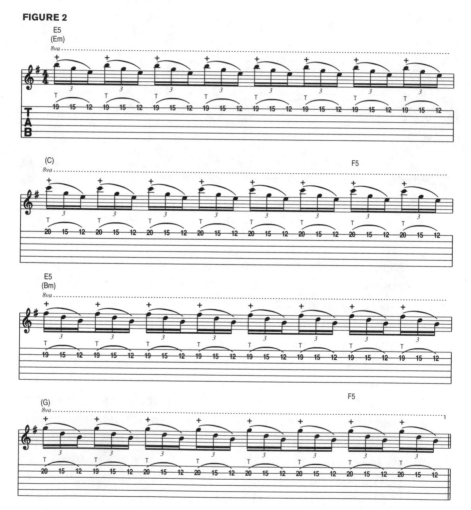

Hammett's tapping technique is a bit different from the ordinary Van Halen-derived approach employed by most mainstream metal guitarists. "I use the middle finger, not the first finger, and pull it off the string after I hit it—down toward the floor instead of up.

I anchor my right hand on the strings, muting them with the lower part of my palm as I tap."

Hammett offered an interesting tap-on variation that is also effective over the same E5-F5 progression **(Figure 3)**. Played entirely on the second string, this lick involves the use of a pedal tone (the high E note). As with the previous example, Hammett deviates slightly from the prevailing modality of the accompaniment, using an F# instead of an F natural. But what the heck—that's polymodality, a trademark of Metallica's sound.

FIGURE 3

Hammett is fond of using "outside" scale/interval lines in his improvisations. **Figure 4** is a perfect example of a fingering pattern gone wild: Hammett creates an atonal impression by stacking unrelated arpeggios momentarily (E major, Bb major and Bb diminished) in an ascending sequence. This lick is similar to one that appears in Hammett's "The Shortest Straw" solo. Notice the symmetrical fretboard shapes throughout. "I actually got it from George Lynch," Hammett confesses with a laugh. "But don't tell him because he'll come knocking on my door demanding money!" Hammett needn't be concerned about any legal Lynch mob, as this pattern appeared as Example 27 in Oliver Nelson's jazz method *Patterns for Saxophone*, published in 1966.

FIGURE 4

Figure 5 is a slight departure for Hammett. Much like a phrase in "The God That Failed," the lick has a droning, sitar-like quality created by the alternating open first-string notes and fretted 2nd-string notes. "It was originally influenced by the Rolling Stones' 'Paint It Black,' " notes Hammett. "It has the D# in it, so I hear it as being in E harmonic-minor [*E-F#-G-A-B-C-D#*]. I use just the middle finger for the whole thing, sliding it up and down the neck. I think that gives the line greater continuity. The picking is all back-and-forth—down on the second string, up on the first."

FIGURE 5

FIGURE 6

Mixing modes within a line is a Kirk Hammett signature. The licks in **Figure 6**, similar to his solo in "Sad but True," are practically textbook in this regard. Here, Hammett combines E major with various modal sounds (E minor-pentatonic, E Dorian and E Aeolian) in a tight, self-contained phrase. "I love the oscillation I hear when I slide the minor thirds up. Going to the blues and pentatonic stuff right afterward creates a cool contrast. That part has a sort of Tony Iommi or Eric Clapton feel to it. I start mixing the modes in the descending section and end with a pinch harmonic. To me, the whole thing feels like a complete sentence.

FIGURE 7

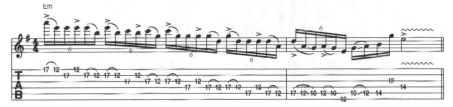

"One new thing I've been working on lately is wide stretches [*perfect fourths*] inside the standard pentatonic positions. This is kind of like what I do in 'Don't Tread on Me' **(Figure 7)**. It could work over E5 and maybe F5—it suggests F minor—but it's really what I would use in a break with just the drums going. The pattern is like that Jimmy Page triplet thing, only I'm using a wider finger stretch. That's how I look at it. This is a weird lick—I can only play it fast! When I play it slow, it sounds confusing as hell because of all the unison notes. I need to hear the flow of the rhythm." That's never a problem in Metallica.

GUITAR WORLD, OCTOBER 1991

RIFFER MADNESS

The hows, whys and wherefores of
the heaviest riffs known to man.
By Wolf Marshall

THRASH TITAN JAMES Hetfield is the driving guitar force behind the heavy thunder of Metallica. Raised on a steady diet of Black Sabbath, Ted Nugent, Aerosmith, Thin Lizzy and AC/DC, he is obsessed with rhythm and lives by the golden rule, "If you ain't got a riff, you ain't got a song." Accordingly, James has been responsible for some of the most earthshaking and influential rhythm grooves in modern metal. Consumed with the task of putting the final touches on the soon-to-be-unleashed fifth Metallica record, he broke free to discuss his inimitable approach to metal rhythm playing and riff-making—and what it takes to destroy the listener with a handful of power chords.

Hetfield jumped right in with an intense galloping figure à la "Battery," illustrating many of his trademark rhythm techniques **(Figure 1)**. This solid, propulsive riff is based on the characteristic speed metal rhythm. "Though I play a lot of all-downstroke rhythms," says Hetfield, "I use alternate picking for this kind of part; at this speed, you pretty much have to! I hold my pick in what might seem like a strange way—with three fingers [*thumb, index and middle fingers*]. I've always written in that position—holding a pencil with three fingers. I guess it evolved from that. It gives me more

FIGURE 1

power—I can't really hang onto it any other way—and it flattens out the pick a little more too. I think the pick being flatter on the string makes things more 'grindy.' Parts of my fingers hit the string [*adding extra texture and crunch*]. I've got a giant callous from scraping. My nail doesn't quite grow correctly either, especially on tour. I mute a lot with my right-hand palm and with my left-hand fingers or thumb."

Another aspect of this figure, and of Metallica's music and speed metal in general, is its unmistakable harmonic movement—the stylistic tritone relationship of Bb5 to E (the flat five interval), the infamous "Diabolus in Musica" of the Middle Ages. "I don't know if it's medieval," grins Hetfield, "but it's definitely evil. They used to hang you for stuff like this! Sabbath was a major influence earlier in my life, and those sounds were the most evil things I heard in their songs. Those notes, those chords—the darker sounds, I suppose—go back to Sabbath, and they're still with me."

Notice Hetfield's use of chromaticism in the figure: Bb5 to A5 and Em to D# diminished diads. Again, this is an element frequently encountered in thrash.

Figure 2 is a perfect example of the type of efficient, but unorthodox, chord fingerings required to play today's hyper-speed metal effectively. Hetfield has developed some interesting left-hand structures to facilitate quick, accurate motion when switching between power chords. For the quick alternation between the E5 and Bb5 chords, Hetfield employs two forms that enable his hand to remain in one position (at the first fret) throughout the riff **(Figure 3)**. Note that the E5 chord is fingered with a second-finger barre and that the Bb5 involves index finger and pinky fretting. "I use these

FIGURE 2

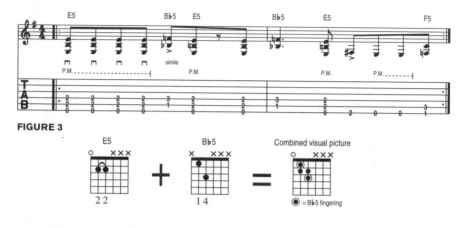

FIGURE 3

Combined visual picture

two shapes a lot," says Hetfield. "It's easier than moving the same shape around to different positions. This one's all downstrokes with muting." Again, check out the tritone (E5 to Bb5) and half-step movement in the example (E5 to F5).

Figure 4, which is similar to a Hetfield riff in "Shortest Straw," incorporates successive downstrokes, alternate picking, half-step movement, palm muting, single notes (see bar 1) and chords. The single-note section involves sliding and bending. "I think of these lines as bass-note-ish—something you might play along with the bass. Originally, this riff was in D; I had the guitar tuned down a whole step. I could bend the strings a lot easier, but it sounded a little too muddy, so I moved it up to E."

FIGURE 4

Along similar lines is the riff illustrated in **Figure 5**. The melody's E Phrygian modality (E-F-G-A-B-C-D) in the first two bars has a bit of a Spanish quality. Notice the trill ("That's straight from

FIGURE 5

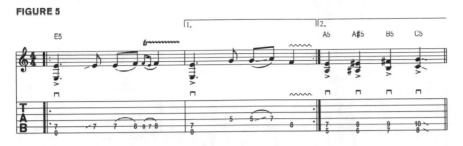

Tony Iommi"), slides and vibrato in this portion of the figure. The climbing chromatic power chords (A5-A#5-B5-C5) of the closing cadence are a Metallica trademark. "When you look at some of the other regular metal tunes, you say, 'Why even have these frets?' The way I see it, you gotta use some of the shit," he says with a laugh. "I like the half-step kind of movement anyway—it builds up a part or it can take it down. It's on its way somewhere."

Our final example **(Figure 6)** is related to the fingering efficiency touched upon in **Figures 2** and **3**. Here, a classic rock chord progression—E5 to G5—is subjected to Hetfield's economy-of-motion principle. Note the first-finger barre for the E5 chord and the middle-finger-and-pinky form for the G5 **(Figure 7)**. This fingering provides a fixed second-position placement for both voicings—a real advantage when negotiating the breakneck tempos of speed metal. Though this move demands a bit of left-hand stretching and some extra pinky strength, it's well worth the effort.

FIGURE 6

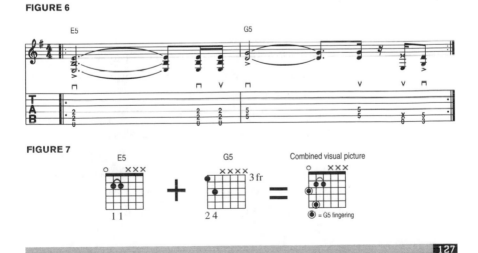

GUITAR WORLD, MARCH 1992

ENTER HANDMAN

Kirk Hammett demonstrates some of the wide-stretch runs and precision exercises that made him 1991's "Best Heavy Metal Guitarist."

By Nick Bowcott

NOW THAT METALLICA has made the rock world safe for thrash guitarists everywhere, more and more attention is being focused on the wide-ranging skills of Kirk Hammett. Fortunately for *Guitar World* and its readers, Hammett's growing popularity has not diminished his enthusiasm for sharing his ample six-string expertise. In the following lesson, Hammett offers precision-picking practice pointers, several serpentine, wide-stretch licks and runs and a host of personal insights. Also included in this exclusive lesson are several exercises taught to Hammett by his guitar guru, Joe Satriani.

We caught up with Hammett just after he and Metallica concluded a marathon two-and-a-half-hour set. What would have zapped the strength of most guitarists left the thoroughbred thrasher full of pep and raring to rock.

"A great way of zoning in on your picking technique is to do this [*plays Figure 1*] or this [*plays Figure 2*]," says Hammett. "Both exercises function as excellent right-hand warm-ups. Because your left hand is idle, you can really concentrate on your picking form. If you concentrate on pivoting from the wrist rather than the elbow, your whole picking movement can be made extremely pre-

FIGURE 1

FIGURE 2

cise, controlled and economical. I recommend practicing the two exercises using alternate picking and all down strokes. This will help you develop speed and strength for intense rhythm work.

"I also recommend practicing this one-handed idea using all six strings **[Figure 3]**. This will help any player get accustomed to moving fluently between strings when picking at high speed. If you have a metronome, use it here to help develop some precision.

FIGURE 3

"Next, I'd like to show you a cool alternate picking and left/right-hand coordination exercise that Joe Satriani taught me," Hammett continues. "Basically, I'm just taking a fingering pattern and moving it across the neck as far as it can go and then back again **[Figure 4]**. It's pretty tough to play this one quickly, due to the

FIGURE 4

(use strict alternate picking throughout)

amount of string skipping involved.

"This next little exercise [*Figure 5*] is good for loosening up and strengthening your left hand—especially your little finger," says Kirk. "It may seem like a bit of nothing, but if you take it from the high E string to the low E string and then back again a number of times, you'll definitely feel it in your fingers!

FIGURE 5

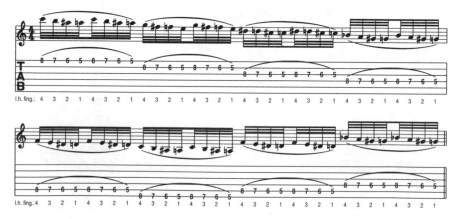

"This next pattern [*Figure 6*] will help improve your hammering-on strength. This is another relatively simple idea, but it does a number on your left hand! As your left-hand fingers become stronger, you should try taking this run all the way from the first position to the 12th and then back again." While only six bars of

FIGURE 6

this run are written out in Figure 6, Hammett continued this pattern all the way to the 12th position.

"Joe [*Satriani*] once showed me a trilling exercise [***Figure 7***] that's a real mother! It looks extremely simple but is actually very hard. It forces you to expand your reach. Increasing the space between your fingers like this makes each trill more and more difficult. I don't do this one very often—I mean, it's ridiculous, man!"

FIGURE 7

Although Hammett demonstrated this excruciating piece of digital torture in the third position, in consideration of your precious fingers, I've transcribed it in the seventh position. Once you've mastered this, I suggest you start playing the exercise closer to the nut, moving down one fret at a time. You'll find that this exercise will strengthen your left hand considerably, and make wide stretches easier too; all you need is patience and perseverance. Be extremely careful when playing this figure—don't risk injury by overexerting yourself, and never attempt it unless your left hand is well and truly warmed up. Also, as Hammett was quick to point out, you should practice this "mother" on every string.

Hammett closed his informative tutorial by playing five runs and licks that handily demonstrate the benefits of left-hand development and digital "stretchability." **Figure 8** is similar to something in the "…And Justice for All" solo, and uses the E Dorian (E-F#-G-A-B-C#-D) and E minor-blues scales (E-G-A-Bb-B-D). (Note: The lead break in question is actually in F# minor, but Hammett elected to play it here in E minor). **Figure 9** is also in E minor. Notice how it requires the player to perform the same wide stretch (12th fret to the 17th) on the first, second, third, fourth and fifth strings.

FIGURE 8

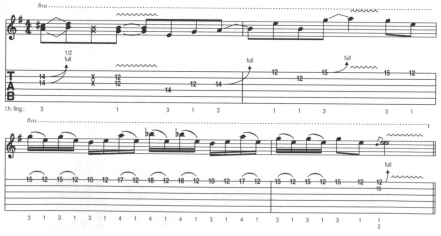

FIGURE 9

"This one is based on a lick I do in my lengthy, 'regurgitating' lead in 'My Friend of Misery' [*from the* Metallica *album*]," notes Hammett, playing **Figure 10**, an F# minor blues scale (F#-A-B-C-C#-E) ditty. "Every time I hear that solo, it reminds me of someone going through a long torturous barf! Next is a melodic, Hendrix-influenced E minor lick [*Figure 11*] similar to one I do at the end of 'Enter Sandman,' though you can hardly hear it because of the fade.

FIGURE 10

FIGURE 11

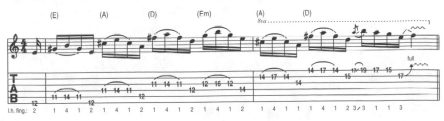

"This final run [*Figure 12*] is something I came up with a couple of years ago, but haven't been able to get onto an album yet. It's a stacked-arpeggio-type thing that involves some string-skipping, and a lot of hammering-on and pulling-off with your pinky." For your convenience, I've indicated the "stacked arpeggios" above the figure. You may notice that I haven't given this run a specific key signature. It will definitely work over an E5 power chord.

FIGURE 12

Metallica in '86 with Cliff Burton

Krasner & Trebitz/Ebet Roberts

METALLICA TIMELINE

A chronological history of the mighty Metallica.

1982

June 14—*Metal Massacre*, a Metal Blade Records compilation, is released. Features "Hit the Lights," the first recording by Metallica (James Hetfield, vocals/rhythm guitar/bass; Lars
Ulrich, drums; Dave Mustaine, lead guitar; Lloyd Grant, lead guitar).

1983

January 7—Bassist Ron McGovney leaves the band—Cliff Burton
of Trauma is selected as Metallica's new bassist.
April 11—Lead guitarist Dave Mustaine is fired.
April 16—Exodus guitarist Kirk Hammett joins Metallica.
Summer—Metallica's debut album, *Kill 'Em All*, is released on
Megaforce Records.
July 27—September 3—Metallica co-headlines the "Kill 'Em All
for One" tour with label-mates Raven.
December—Metallica plays a series of headlining gigs on the East
Coast with Anthrax.

1984

January and February—Metallica fills support slot on Venom's

European "Seven Dates of Hell" tour.

Mid-February—Band unsuccessfully attempts to persuade Armored Saint vocalist John Bush to join Metallica.

February 11—Metallica plays Zwolle, Holland Aardschok Festival, before 5,000 people, their largest audience to date.

February 20—*Jump in the Fire* EP released in Europe. Metallica begins work on their second album, *Ride the Lightning*, at Sweet Silence studios in Copenhagen, Denmark.

March 14—Metallica makes its first UK appearance, at London's Marquee Club (followed by an encore show there on March 27).

June 6—Mini-European tour (the band's second that year) starts in Leiden, Holland, with Twisted Sister.

August 12—Megaforce Management (Jon & Marsha Zazula) out, Q-Prime Management (Cliff Burnstein & Peter Mensch) in. Metallica signs U.S. deal with Elektra Records (in Europe, they continue with Music for Nations, the company they'd been licensed to through Megaforce since the release of *Kill 'Em All*).

November 16—*Ride the Lightning* re-released by Elektra.

November 23—*Creeping Death* EP released in Europe.

December 20—Metallica performs at the Lyceum; headlines London for the first time.

1985

January 10—U.S. co-headline tour with WASP begins in Nova Scotia (and ends in Portland, Oregon, on 3/19. Midway through the tour, WASP breaks off the bill and Armored Saint jumps in to open for Metallica).

August 17—Band plays at Castle Donnington's "Monsters of Rock" Festival in UK for first time, before 70,000 people.

September 2—Recording sessions for *Master of Puppets* commence in Copenhagen, Denmark.

September 30—Metallica plays "Day on the Green" Festival in Oakland, California, before 80,000 people.

1986

February 21—*Master of Puppets* released in U.S.

March 27—"Damage, Inc." U.S. tour (opening for Ozzy Osbourne) starts in Wichita, Kansas (and ends in Hampton, VA, on 8/3).

September 10—European leg of "Damage, Inc." tour begins in Cardiff, Wales.

September 26—Last gig with Cliff Burton in Stockholm, Sweden.

September 27—Cliff Burton dies in tour bus accident in Sweden.

October 28—Jason Newsted joins band.

November 8—Metallica plays first gig with Jason Newsted at L.A.'s Country Club.

November 10—Band plays five dates on mini-tour of Japan.

November 15—Another mini-tour, this time in Canada and the Pacific Northwest, with openers Metal Church.

1987

February 8—"Damage, Inc." world tour officially ends in Zwolle, Holland.

July—Recording sessions for *The 5.98 EP* begin in Los Angeles, California.

August 21—*The 5.98 EP* released in America.

December 4—*Cliff 'Em All* home video released in U.S.

1988

January 15—*Kill 'Em All* re-released in U.S. on Elektra with two bonus tracks.

January 29—Recording sessions for *...And Justice for All* begin in L.A.

May 27—"Monsters of Rock" tour begins in East Troy, Wisconsin—with 40,000 people in attendance.

August 25—*...And Justice for All* released in America (LP spawns subsequent singles "Harvester of Sorrow," "One," and "Eye of the Beholder").

September 11—First show on "Damaged Justice" tour takes place in Budapest, Hungary.

November 15—U.S. leg of "Damaged Justice" tour starts in Toledo, Ohio.

December 6—Band shoots footage for "One" video in L.A.

1989

February 22—Group performs "One" live at the Grammy Awards.

May 3—Band plays Australia for the first time at Abelaide's Theater.

1990

October—Recording sessions for *Metallica* album begin at One on One Studios in Los Angeles with producer Bob Rock.

1991

August 12—*Metallica* is released.

1992

February—Metallica performs "Enter Sandman" at Grammy Awards; wins Grammy for Best Metal Performance.

August 9—James Hetfield suffers second-degree burns on his face, arms, hands and legs after walking into a flashpot during a Montreal concert

November—*A Year and a Half in the Life of Metallica* home video is released.

1993

November 29—Box set *Live Shit: Binge & Purge*, containing three CDs, three videos and a book, is released.

1995

December—Band begins recording *Load* with producer Bob Rock.

1996

June 4—*Load* is released.

June 27—Metallica headlines Lollapalooza festival.

GUITAR WORLD

PRESENTS

Guitar World Presents is an ongoing series of books filled with extraordinary interviews, feature pieces and instructional material that have made *Guitar World* magazine the world's most popular musicians' magazine. For years, *Guitar World* has brought you the most timely, the most accurate and the most hard-hitting news and views about your favorite players. Now you can have it all in one convenient package: *Guitar World Presents.*

Guitar World Presents Classic Rock
00330370 (304 pages, 6" x 9") $17.95

Guitar World Presents Alternative Rock
00330369 (352 pages, 6" x 9") $17.95

Guitar World Presents Nirvana and the Grunge Revolution
00330368 (240 pages, 6" x 9") $16.95

Guitar World Presents Kiss
00330291 (144 pages, 6" x 9") $14.95

Guitar World Presents Van Halen
00330294 (208 pages, 6" x 9") $14.95

Guitar World Presents Metallica
00330292 (144 pages, 6" x 9") $14.95

Guitar World Presents Stevie Ray Vaughan
00330293 (144 pages, 6" x 9") $14.95

FOR MORE INFORMATION, SEE YOUR LOCAL MUSIC DEALER, OR WRITE TO:

HAL•LEONARD®
CORPORATION

7777 W. BLUEMOUND RD. P.O. BOX 13819 MILWAUKEE, WI 53213

Prices and availability subject to change without notice.
Some products may not be available outside the U.S.A.